ASBURY PARK
❦ REBORN ❧

ASBURY PARK

❧ REBORN ☙

Lost to Time and Restored to Glory

⋯ JOSEPH G. BILBY & HARRY ZIEGLER ⋯

THE
History
PRESS

Published by The History Press
Charleston, SC 29403
www.historypress.net

First published 2012

Manufactured in the United States

ISBN 978.1.60949.680.7

Library of Congress CIP data applied for.

Notice: The information in this book is true and complete to the best of our knowledge. It is offered without guarantee on the part of the authors or The History Press. The authors and The History Press disclaim all liability in connection with the use of this book.

CONTENTS

CONTENTS

Sources and Acknowledgements

Anyone with an interest in the history of Asbury Park cannot begin to investigate it without consulting Helen-Chantel Pike's now classic work, *Asbury Park's Glory Days: The Story of an American Resort*. Daniel Wolfe's *4th of July Asbury Park: A History of the Promised Land*, a thematically arranged history, is another modern classic. Madonna Carter Jackson's *Asbury Park: A West Side Story—A Pictorial Journey Through the Eyes of Joseph A. Carter Sr.* is an essential guide to the story of the city's African American community, and Kathy A. Kelly's *Asbury Park's Ghosts and Legends* is a must-read for those with a bent for the paranormal. We also suggest a visit to the Asbury Park Historical Society website (www.aphistoricalsociety.org), which provides abundant information about past and current projects on the history of Asbury Park and the preservation of its past. Of course, the authors would also humbly suggest our own book from The History Press, *Asbury Park: A Brief History*. We have consulted all of those works in the writing of this guidebook. In addition, we have combed back issues of a variety of newspapers, most notably the *Asbury Park Press* and the *New York Times*, the latter providing a surprisingly complete record of Asbury Park events in the nineteenth and early twentieth centuries, a period when the *Times* and other New York City newspapers covered New Jersey like a blanket.

To supplement the historical sources, we have also interviewed a number of people who have witnessed Asbury Park history in the making and have a special interest in preserving and remembering the city's past, including events surrounding the sites described in this book. Special thanks are also due to Asbury Park librarians Robert Stewart and Malakia Oglesby; Don Stine, president of the Asbury Park Historical Society; Judy Feinstein and James Kaufman of Flying Saucers; Kathy A. Kelly of Paranormal Books; Brian Boyce and Lou Parisi of VFW Post 1333; Clark McCullough and Robert V. McKnight of the George A. Custer Camp #17, Sons of Union Veterans; and former Neptune Township school administrator Bob Pontecorvo. If there is anyone we have forgotten, please accept our apologies, as it was unintentional.

INTRODUCTION

Any city worth the name that has endured the test of time for a century and more has its iconic sites—locations and buildings that tell its story. Asbury Park, a world-famous resort on the New Jersey coast, best known in the modern era for its relationship with rock-and-roll music in general and Bruce Springsteen in particular but boasting a rather unique past, is no exception. From its inception as a resort for middle-class white Protestant Americans (who needed a significant black working class to ensure their vacation comfort) in the mind of its eccentric founder, the mercurial James A. Bradley, through its twentieth-century ups and downs under leaders like Mayor Clarence Hetrick and a somewhat less colorful cast of successors, Asbury Park has seen many of its historic buildings demolished, despite their historic merit. A surprising number have endured, however, and most, although regrettably not all, of the sites we describe in this book still stand, although their uses have changed, often dramatically, over the years. The nineteenth- to mid-twentieth-century sites covered in the book range from commemorative statues to buildings used, at one time or another, as banks, armories, a national political headquarters, newspaper offices and, it being Asbury Park, several iconic rock-and-roll performance venues.

Each site is provided, in addition to a brief but comprehensive essay on its unique history and current use, with an address, GPS location and, when available, links to websites that provide more detailed information and relevant film clips. We have divided the sites into three separate tours, based on proximity. Sites are grouped based on both adjacent locations and the unfolding of the Asbury Park story, starting with the memorial statue to James A. Bradley and ending with the Civil War monument, the only one of its kind in a Monmouth County shore community.

Asbury Park's diverse array of architectural landmarks creates an unforgettable impression of this legendary seaside city and provides fascinating evidence on the city's past, present and even future. Buildings like the elegant, Art Deco–inspired Convention Hall and Casino capture the resort's glittering heyday in the 1920s and 1930s, while structures such as the former Upstage Club in the heart of downtown reflect an era when aspiring musicians like Bruce Springsteen played at intimate venues and helped to define Asbury's world-renowned music scene.

We hope this guidebook will take readers on a journey through the colorful history of a remarkable resort, as revealed by the eclectic architectural gems that represent various aspects of the city's story. From opulent movie houses to down-and-dirty rock-and-roll clubs, these landmarks, some gone and some saved, trace the evolution of Asbury Park from a tiny nineteenth-century resort town with big ambition on the then-desolate shores of Monmouth County, New Jersey, to the world-famous playground of today. As the city moves ahead in its ambitious redevelopment plans, many neglected buildings have been rehabilitated into impressive new venues, but others, sadly, continue to deteriorate or have been destroyed, often despite a groundswell of public opposition. This book includes both preservation successes and failures, hoping for more of the former than the latter in the future.

Tour 1

NORTH ASBURY

JAMES A. BRADLEY STATUE

Located in the park across Ocean Avenue from Convention Hall
GPS: 40° 13' 26.62" N, 73° 59' 59.35" W

"I would have been much happier in my old age had I never heard of the place." So the mercurial James A. Bradley, revered as "the Founder" of Asbury Park, reputedly said in his declining years. Even so, the city erected a commemorative statue of Bradley in 1921, within weeks of his demise on June 1 of that year. The statue still stands, its unseeing eyes staring at Convention Hall, the Art Deco masterpiece erected within a decade of the Founder's passing. One wonders what Bradley would think today, as the culture of this city by the sea does not remotely reflect either the quasi-theocratic future he envisioned for his creation in 1871 or the long-lost world he was born into on February 14, 1830, at Staten Island's Blazing Star tavern. Sometimes people indeed live too long.

The James A. Bradley statue erected in 1921 shortly after the Asbury Park Founder's death. *Courtesy of the Asbury Park Library.*

James A. Bradley was a self-made man in true nineteenth-century mode. Born into humble circumstances as the son of an alcoholic father who died prematurely, he rejected the gang culture of lower Manhattan that he grew up in and apprenticed himself as a young man to a brush manufacturer, rising to the rank of shop foreman, marrying a woman who proved a steady helpmate and becoming a teetotaling Methodist along the way. Bradley saved his money, eventually opened his own brush factory and, with hard work and luck, steered the fledgling business through the Panic (the nineteenth-century equivalent of a depression) of 1857 and then made an enormous amount of money supplying brushes of all sorts to the Union army during the Civil War.

Even with his considerable success, all of Bradley's business ups and downs apparently brought him to a state of what was then called "nervous exhaustion" by 1870. A New York City friend recommended a vacation home in the then-new Methodist "Camp Meeting" resort of Ocean Grove, and Bradley became one of the first investors in the town. He found release from his cares, and his probable clinical depression, on the Jersey Shore, lying naked on the beach while the incoming tide lapped around him. Bradley also envisioned, in the then-barren coastal landscape north of Ocean Grove, a project that would combine his religious idealism and business sense. Smitten by the shore, he mortgaged his brush company for the $90,000 needed to buy the property and was off on a new adventure.

Within a year, Bradley had graduated from Ocean Grove property owner to the Founder of Asbury Park, which he named for eighteenth-century Methodist bishop and missionary Francis Asbury. Creating the new resort city

Although the surrounding area has changed significantly, the Bradley statue has remained in the same spot since 1921. *Courtesy of Joseph Bilby.*

adjacent to the camp meeting town was a logical leap for Bradley, as he entered an enthusiastic "up" phase in his long journey through life. Although devout, Bradley saw his creation as sort of an "Ocean Grove light" municipality, with the prohibition of alcohol and strict moral code of the camp meeting resort but with less of the twenty-four-hour pervasive religious atmosphere then characteristic of its neighbor. The new resort was aimed at a growing population of post–Civil War American middle-class families, courted by Bradley to take a journey by train to enjoy a wholesome week by the sea as the New York and Long Branch Railroad worked its way south along the coast.

Albeit religiously conservative and paternalistic, Bradley was also somewhat progressive, and in Asbury Park, he established the first sewage system and appointed the first board of health in any New Jersey Shore town. By 1880, Asbury Park had a permanent "promenade boardwalk," with benches situated every ten feet. The boardwalk, and the beach itself, was adorned with what the somewhat eccentric Bradley considered "educational" exhibits, ranging from old stagecoaches to rusty zoo cages and other esoteric objects. By the mid-1880s, Asbury Park boasted three thousand permanent residents and was host to fifty thousand vacationers each year. By 1888, the city had an electric trolley system and was among the top three vacation spots on the New Jersey Shore, along with Long Branch and Atlantic City. Asbury Park differed dramatically from its competitors, however, in that its appeal was based in its reputation as a middle-class family resort, rather than a honky-tonk gambling venue like Long Branch or a boisterous blue-collar day-trip destination like Atlantic City.

Bradley constantly hovered over public life in Asbury Park, sometimes as the official mayor but always as an almost-omniscient presence, micromanaging his creation. He hired detectives to chase "beer arks," horse-drawn wagons from Neptune and other local municipalities that sold beer to residents and vacationers, and he maintained a personal watch on the resort's amusements to make sure they did not involve games of chance on any level. On one occasion, Bradley smashed a boardwalk "doll game," which he interpreted as a gambling enterprise, with an axe. As a self-appointed enforcer of public morals, the Founder erected a sign forbidding young couples from engaging in the moral hazard of canoeing on Deal Lake at the north end of town—a prohibition that was apparently widely ignored. Bradley's enforcement efforts waxed and waned over the years, however, coinciding with the ups and downs of his enthusiasms, leading a modern observer to speculate that he was probably afflicted with a bipolar personality. On one occasion, he gave up a desperate fight with the traveling beer vendors, pronounced alcohol prohibition an abject failure and took off for the White Mountains of New Hampshire for a long vacation. Within a short time, he was back chasing the arks in what was indeed a largely fruitless effort.

James A. Bradley's Asbury Park unsurprisingly reflected the pervasive racism of nineteenth-century America. The workforce that kept the resort functioning was largely African American. Few of these workers actually lived in Asbury Park, with most residing in the "unincorporated" section of Neptune Township across the railroad tracks to the west, which became part of Asbury Park in the early twentieth century. Bradley imposed beach and boardwalk racial segregation restrictions on the workers so that they wouldn't disturb his white vacationers with their presence during peak tourist daytime hours. This policy was understandably resented by the black community. In 1887, one activist, Reverend James Francis Robinson, evoked the sacrifices of African American men in the Union army, some of whom were no doubt in his audience, to dramatically state his case for racial equality. (Over three thousand black New Jersey men served in the Civil War, and Asbury Park had its own Grand Army of the Republic post for black veterans, the Captain Andrew Cailloux Post Number 119.) This issue resurfaced yearly well into the twentieth century and can be counted as one of the nagging inequality issues that resulted in the civil disturbances that rocked the city in 1970. Characteristically, when the issue became particularly hot, Bradley would absent himself on vacation out of state or in Europe.

As the nineteenth century waned, and he aged, James A. Bradley began to lose his grip on the community's lifestyle. In addition to the traveling beer arks, actual bootlegging became relatively common in the allegedly "dry" town, and an 1892 account described Asbury Park as "essentially a secular community." There would be one last moment of public fame for Bradley and his increasingly quaint view of the world, however. In 1893, he ran for the office of New Jersey state senator, handing out brushes to housewives and dimes to their children as part of his "picturesque" campaign, a practice that was decried by his opposition as out-and-out bribery to affect the votes of husbands and fathers. Bradley won the election and, in his one term in office, provided the deciding vote to ban horse racing in the state, citing his religious antipathy to gambling. Residents of the competing resort of Long Branch, which featured a racetrack as a prime attraction, claimed his vote was less than idealistic.

The end came with a whimper, as Asbury Park's merchants—concerned about the declining condition of the boardwalk, as well as Bradley's deteriorating animal cages and assorted detritus attractions—pressed the Founder to sell the oceanfront, which he personally owned, to the city. In 1903, he did, for $100,000 and accepted an additional $50,000 for his sewer system. In 1906, the city annexed the unincorporated area beyond the railroad tracks. The boardwalk was upgraded. Coney Island–style amusement entrepreneurs came to town. Bradley lived on, a curiosity in a world not of his making, until 1921. And now he maintains an eternal watch on Convention Hall, with the occasional pigeon or seagull for company.

CONVENTION HALL AND THE PARAMOUNT THEATER

1300 Ocean Avenue

732-897-6500

www.youtube.com/watch?v=nH4UAwfWVNk

GPS: 40° 13' 25.53" N, 73° 59' 55.10" W

After taking office as a city commissioner in 1915 and subsequently being elected mayor by his four fellow commissioners, Asbury Park's Clarence Hetrick came to the conclusion that his city by the sea had to compete seriously with Enoch "Nucky" Johnson's Atlantic City to the south for the crown of top year-round tourism center of the Jersey Shore. In order to capture the offseason market Hetrick desired, he needed to attract the then-growing convention business. These gatherings included large, national multiday meetings of

Mayor Clarence Hetrick's Convention Hall as it appeared from the boardwalk in the 1930s. *Courtesy of the Asbury Park Library.*

The interior of Convention Hall, set up for an event, in the 1930s. *Courtesy of the Asbury Park Library.*

business, fraternal and veterans' organizations and were invariably scheduled for a venue that would prove attractive to the membership of those groups, aside from any business transacted. In 1905, the National Education Association had held its convention in Asbury Park and Ocean Grove, and the mayor envisioned a steady stream of such events in the future. He realized, however, that he needed to do a lot of modernizing work in his city to make that happen with regularity. That work would take longer than he thought.

Hetrick needed a modern convention center and believed that he could build one in the northern section of Asbury Park on land then the site of a ramshackle municipal auditorium built by the city's founder, James A. Bradley, in the previous century. Once acquired by the city, thought the mayor, this eyesore could be demolished as an important first step in his plan to bring Asbury Park into the twentieth century. In 1916, Hetrick hired a nationally known architecture firm to design a convention center building for the auditorium lot between Sixth and Sunset Avenues, without consulting Bradley. The Founder's late nineteenth-century Methodist vision of what future Asbury Park should aspire to was in sharp contrast with that of the modernizing mayor, however, and Bradley refused to sell his building and the surrounding property to the city, dooming the plan.

Following Bradley's death in 1921, the property was purchased from his estate by Arthur Steinbach of the city's department store family, who, with a group of fellow investors, subsequently demolished the auditorium and built the Berkeley-Carteret Hotel on the property. Although his original site was now off the table, Hetrick persisted in the idea that his city needed an up-to-date convention center to compete with Atlantic City.

The burned cruise ship *Morro Castle*, which drifted in to the Asbury Park shore off Convention Hall in September 1934 as it was being towed to New York to be scrapped. *Courtesy of the Asbury Park Library.*

The *Morro Castle* memorial tablet erected by the Asbury Park Historical Society in 2009. *Courtesy of Joseph Bilby.*

In the late 1920s, Mayor Hetrick renewed his campaign, pointing out in an *Asbury Park Press* article that Atlantic City had outstripped Asbury Park in the number of its construction projects during that dynamic decade and, most notably, had a huge new convention center on the planning boards. Coincidentally, at about the same time that Hetrick renewed his push for a modernization of Asbury's municipal facilities, mysterious fires destroyed both the Fifth Avenue Pavilion, which dated from 1905, located at the north end of the boardwalk, and the Casino building, constructed in 1903 at the south end of the boardwalk. The city council agreed with the mayor that these structures had to be replaced and rapidly approved a special bond issue to pay for new construction at both locations.

Mayor Hetrick entered into a no-bid contract with Architect Whitney Warren of New York City and his partner, attorney Charles Wetmore. Warren, the architect for Steinbach's Berkeley-Carteret Hotel, specialized in the Beaux-Arts style, perhaps unsurprisingly, since he had studied for a number of years at the École des Beaux-Arts in Paris. Warren and Wetmore was perhaps the most well-known architectural firm of its day, responsible for Grand Central Terminal in New York City among other important projects, many of them involving grand hotels.

Warren designed Asbury Park's Convention Hall complex, with a 3,200-seat capacity, as a Beaux-Arts gem that spanned the boardwalk with a graceful "Grand Concourse" arch with skylights

Convention Hall as seen from the site of the James Bradley statue. *Courtesy of Joseph Bilby.*

Convention Hall as it appears from the boardwalk in 2012. *Courtesy of Joseph Bilby*.

and included an auditorium, as well as the 1,600-seat Paramount Theater on the west side of the boardwalk, later administered by famed theater impresario Walter Reade. The Paramount's grand opening in 1930 drew a number of Hollywood stars of the era, including the Marx brothers and Ginger Rogers.

Both structures are currently on the National Register of Historic Places. The hall itself extended 215 feet over the beach, where it rested on steel pilings. Unfortunately, although Convention Hall was designed to answer Hetrick's call for a year-round attraction, Warren apparently forgot to install a heating system. The mayor's boardwalk grand vision accounted for that, though, and when he contracted with Warren and Wetmore to build a new Casino at the south end of the boardwalk, they added a heating plant just beyond it near the Ocean Grove border that would provide heat for not only the Casino but also Convention Hall and other boardwalk sites, making them more attractive as year-round tourist venues. The combined projects set the city back over $4 million, which was paid for by floating municipal bonds—just before the advent of the Great Depression. Asbury Park still owed money on those bonds over thirty years later.

The new construction, which lasted from 1928 to 1930, accomplished one thing for certain—its very presence provided an assurance that the old Asbury Park of James A. Bradley was gone forever, even symbolically. Bradley's statue still stood, but his former view of the sea was totally blocked by Convention Hall. The first group to use Convention Hall as a meeting venue was the New York Friars' Club in 1931. Hetrick could see great things coming. Unfortunately, the economy was crumbling around him as the Great Depression cast its long shadow over the nation.

Asbury Park's first radio station, WCLP, which was owned by the city's chamber of commerce, moved its studio to the second-floor promenade of the new building, overlooking the ocean, in 1931. It was from this vantage on September 9, 1934, that announcer Tom Burley saw the fire-ravaged cruise ship *Morro Castle*, which had burned off Sea Girt several miles to the south, drift into shore. The burned-out hulk was being towed to New York City to be scrapped when it broke loose in bad weather. It seemed to Burley at the time that the ship would actually collide with the building, but it fortunately grounded on a sandbar slightly offshore. The *Morro Castle* remained lodged there through the winter until it was finally towed north in March 1935. Over the months it remained, the ship became a macabre tourist attraction, welcomed by many merchants for bringing business to the city during the cash-starved Depression. Because of the *Morro Castle* disaster, Asbury Park's Convention Hall became familiar to people around the world, as most photographs of the beached liner featured the building as well. Some charred

The Paramount Theater and Convention Hall in 2012. *Courtesy of Joseph Bilby.*

corpses that remained on the ship were apparently removed to the stage of the Paramount for identification, and Asbury Park's Paranormal Books proprietor Kathy Kelly notes that "strange visual phenomena" and "shadow figures" have been reported on the stage from time to time.

Through the 1940s and 1950s and into the 1960s, Convention Hall remained a popular venue for musical performances. The last big band engagement by Harry James occurred in 1946, but a decade later, rock-and-roll was in Asbury to stay, beginning with appearances by popular 1950s groups Frankie Lymon and the Teenagers, the Platters and others. Unfortunately, Lymon's appearance in 1956 resulted in a number of fistfights that were apparently racial in origin, which local residents blamed on "outsiders" or even the nature of rock-and-roll itself, although they could certainly be explained as a symbol of the racial tension in the city that had its origins in Bradley's segregation policies and would boil over in the climactic 1970 riot.

By the late 1970s, Asbury Park was in a definite decline. There were other, newer, bigger venues for conventions and concerts, and Convention Hall became the scene of camping, boating, fishing and home improvement trade shows. Eventually, these shows left the deteriorating building as well.

Although Convention Hall declined through the years, along with the city of Asbury Park, it maintained contact with the music world as a venue for rock-and-roll performers. In recent years, the convention and theater complex has undergone a good deal of restoration and is returning to its position as the crown jewel of the Asbury Park boardwalk. A dream sequence in the popular HBO series *The Sopranos* reintroduced the classic building to a public that had long forgotten it. Bruce Springsteen, loyal to the city that gave him his start, has often used the hall for tour rehearsals, and it is once again reverberating to the sound of music on a regular basis. Jersey Shore Roller Girls, a roller derby team, now calls Convention Hall home as well. The Paramount featured the Gilbert and Sullivan operetta *HMS Pinafore* and the Verdi opera *Il Trovatore* on its stage in the summer of 2012. The Convention Hall complex is a prime example for those who posit that, although Asbury Park has been down, it was never out and is definitely on its way back up.

THE BERKELEY-CARTERET HOTEL, NOW THE BERKELEY OCEANFRONT HOTEL

1401 Ocean Avenue
www.berkeleyhotelnj.com
GPS: 40° 13' 30.14" N, 73° 59' 58.07" W

For hard-driving businessman Arthur C. Steinbach, the evening of June 30, 1925, was undoubtedly one of the most memorable episodes in his life. At a gala event attended by some five hundred influential colleagues from around the state of New Jersey, he presented his architectural masterpiece: the spectacular, eight-story Berkeley-Carteret, a luxury hotel that epitomized elegant vacationing in Asbury Park.

The Berkeley-Carteret, elegantly named for the two British lords who briefly owned colonial New Jersey through a grant from King Charles II, was Steinbach's obsession. He wanted to build the biggest luxury hotel in Asbury Park, one that would dwarf the competition and epitomize the glamour of holiday travel. His vision still stands today, dominating the city's waterfront and representing the vitality and success of Asbury Park's twenty-first-century renaissance.

Certainly, Steinbach must have felt triumphant on the night of the Berkeley-Carteret's public unveiling. He undoubtedly was an exuberant man when he spoke to the crowd that evening, joined by fellow speakers who included United States senator and former New Jersey governor Edward I. Edwards and Asbury Park's mayor, Clarence Hetrick. Guests were treated to a sumptuous banquet in the Meadow Grill and admired the elegance of rooms such as the banquet hall, with its iridescent chandeliers and rose-colored carpet. Even the *New York Times* announced the event, describing the Berkeley-Carteret as the "newest and largest hotel" in Asbury Park.

For Steinbach, construction of the Berkeley-Carteret was yet another professional milestone in a life dominated by ambition and achievement. He was the son of another prominent local entrepreneur, John Steinbach, who had opened the legendary Steinbach's department store in Asbury Park. The elder Steinbach's wife, Eugenia, had two children, Arthur and Walter, before her death shortly after Walter's birth. The grief-stricken husband never remarried. Instead, the elder Steinbach threw himself into the business, leaving the care of his sons to the family help, with the housekeeper "Noanie" in charge. As his sons grew into manhood,

The Berkeley-Carteret Hotel in the 1930s. *Courtesy of the Asbury Park Library.*

The Berkeley-Carteret Hotel in 2012. The hotel declined over the years but has been restored to its former glory. *Courtesy of Joseph Bilby.*

Walter became an intellectual philanthropist who thought nothing of dispensing his time and money to help the needy, while Arthur evolved into a consummate, profit-oriented businessman, precise and rigid in his ways. While Walter hobnobbed with members of the Lost Generation in the Paris literary scene of the 1920s, Arthur focused on expanding his family's holdings and became obsessed with the building and decorating of the Berkeley-Carteret, in which he held a significant financial stake.

Steinbach had quietly negotiated with the estate of resort founder James A. Bradley to purchase the tract on which the city's dilapidated Auditorium remained after the Founder's death. To build his architectural masterpiece, Steinbach hired Whitney Warren and his lawyer partner, Charles Wetmore. Their firm was known for designing large hotels, and their work in New York included Grand Central Terminal and a cluster of nearby hotels, including the Biltmore, Commodore and Ambassador. After World War I, the partners were entrusted with designing the reconstruction of the historic library of the Catholic University of Louvain, Belgium, which had been destroyed by the Germans.

Warren drew a cross-shaped design for the Berkeley-Carteret, which, at eight stories, dwarfed its competition. Built by the Turner Construction Company of Philadelphia, the hotel was constructed of steel and concrete and faced in red brick. From the second-floor mezzanine, doors opened to a footbridge that crossed Ocean Avenue, connecting to a new boardwalk pavilion also designed by Warren.

With its more than four hundred rooms, each with baths and showers that featured both fresh and salt water running from the faucets, the Berkeley-Carteret represented the best in luxury and comfort. For Steinbach, maintaining that reputation of impeccable service and quality was imperative. The detail-oriented investor maintained his own living quarters at the hotel so he could keep a close eye on operations. "It was told that he once fired a bellboy for having dirty shoes," recalled Nancy Gibson Harvey, Walter Steinbach's grandniece. "He also gave careful thought to how every room should be made up. He would spell it all out to the maids: 'Make the bed first. Then, even if there is more work to be done, the guest can at least put his suitcase down in his own room. Do the rest after that.'"

The glamour and opulence of the 1920s and 1930s at the Berkeley-Carteret gave way to practicality during the dark days of World War II, when hotels throughout Asbury Park were requisitioned to serve as barracks for military men. The navy leased the Berkeley-Carteret and Monterey Hotels and turned them into "in transit" quarters for British and Commonwealth sailors between ship assignments crewing lend-lease vessels. Sixth Avenue between the two hotels served as a parade ground for morning drills, and at night, the Salvation Army canteen handed out hot cocoa at the Berkeley-Carteret.

Following the war, Steinbach was intent on a return to luxury. Borrowing money from his brother, he refurbished the hotel and built an outdoor pool lined with cabanas. He continued to dote on his pet project, even hanging paintings from his own extensive American art collection on hotel walls. With Steinbach's death in 1954, however, the Berkeley-Carteret lost its strong guiding hand, and the hotel was destined to change hands several times during the 1950s and 1960s. Although the hotel underwent numerous renovations during the period, including the addition of an indoor pool and spa, no amount of cosmetic change could intrigue an increasingly fickle public. Tourists were bypassing Asbury Park and cruising down the Garden State Parkway to newer, more exciting resorts, now made more easily accessible by the new road. In addition, roadside motels represented the younger generation's more informal approach to vacationing; the Berkeley-Carteret was becoming a rather staid reminder of an earlier age. By 1976, the hotel was closed, its guest rooms eerily silent and its once-elegant convention rooms gathering dust.

Fresh hope arrived in the mid-1980s, when brothers Henry and Sebastian Vaccaro restored the structure. Unfortunately, the brothers and their fellow investors ended up in bankruptcy, and the grand old hotel once again went through a revolving door of owners. In 1994, the organization affiliated with Maharishi Maheshi Yogi bought the property, intending to use the hotel as a transcendental meditation university and holistic healthcare center. The Asbury Park city fathers were upset at the plans and disallowed these uses, and the Maharishi had to maintain the structure as an ordinary hotel.

Queens-based entrepreneur Daniel Ahn offered some stability when he purchased and refurbished the building in 1998, keeping it open through the years that the city's new waterfront plans were being created and approved. In 2007, the Berkeley-Carteret moved another step forward with its $16 million purchase by New York real estate investors Joseph and Jacob Chetrit. The brothers, who had substantial real estate holdings around the country, vowed to move quickly on revitalizing the massive property. Their efforts coincided with a waterfront redevelopment project coordinated by Madison Marquette, and during the next several years, both efforts thrived.

Known today as the Berkeley Oceanfront Hotel, the elegant and well-maintained building is once again a well-regarded vacation stop and convention center, billing itself as a "premier boutique hotel offering our guests modern luxury just steps from the famed boardwalk." Its spacious convention rooms are filled with events that range from breathtaking weddings to colorful Halloween parties. Guests dine at the hotel's Dauphin Grille or amble contentedly across Ocean Avenue to the bustling boardwalk, as in days of old.

Certainly Arthur Steinbach, proud patriarch of his beloved Berkeley-Carteret, would be pleased.

HOWARD JOHNSON'S BOARDWALK RESTAURANT, NOW TIM MCLOONE'S SUPPER CLUB AND ASBURY GRILLE

1200 Ocean Avenue

www.timmcloonessupperclub.com

GPS: 40° 13' 23.92" N, 73° 59' 56.55" W

To the older folks who, as children in the post–World War II era, piled into the un-air-conditioned car for a family road trip, the name Howard Johnson's evokes memories of a long-gone America. Howard Johnson's was the first national restaurant chain, dominating the rest stops on the new turnpikes and interstates that heralded the vast expansion of the national road system in the postwar era. Although far from gourmet fare, the chain's dependably consistent food, coupled with its truly outstanding ice cream, available in "28 flavors," gave it iconic status among middle-class Americans. In recent years, that status was conveyed to nostalgic oldsters and a no doubt bemused younger generation via an episode in the fifth season of the popular AMC television series *Mad Men*, when advertising executive Don Draper and his wife, Megan, visit an upstate New York Howard Johnson's in 1966 in search of a new account. The visit leads to domestic turmoil, but not before Don and Megan sample some of the chain's best-known menu items—orange sherbet and fried clams.

Perhaps surprisingly to some in an era of fabricated brand names, Howard Johnson's was indeed founded by a man named Howard Johnson. In the early 1920s, Johnson, a young World War I veteran and Massachusetts native, owned a less than prosperous quasi-pharmacy selling "patent medicines"—non-prescription drugs that had seen a regulatory squeeze (no more opium and alcohol in "tonics," alas) from the federal government in the previous decade. In 1925, almost broke, he tried out a new recipe

Convention Hall (left) and Howard Johnson's (right) in the 1960s. *Courtesy of the Asbury Park Library.*

formula in his adjunct soda fountain and ice cream parlor, doubling the ice cream's butterfat component and adding a number of new flavors. As word got out, Johnson's ice cream customer numbers soared, his business became profitable and he began to plan an expansion. And then the stock market crash of 1929 hit home. Johnson, down but never out, partnered with Harold Sprague, and the two men came up with the idea of franchising his brand. The company began an extensive franchise expansion during the 1930s, despite the Depression. By the beginning of World War II, there were more than one hundred Howard Johnson's restaurants, either franchised or directly owned by the company. Although Massachusetts had the most "HoJo's" of any state, there were some as far away as Florida.

The war, with its food and gas rationing and travel restrictions, put a severe crimp in the burgeoning chain, and by 1946,

Johnson, who had managed to preserve some of his revenue stream by selling food to war workers at defense plants, was still almost bankrupt. He fought his way back once more, however, adding motel accommodations to many restaurant locations in the early 1950s, which was when a newly prosperous and mobile American middle class discovered that the chain's comfortable and consistent quality food and its twenty-eight flavors of ice cream, along with available lodging at many locations, made it an ideal stop on a road trip for lunch, dinner and/or overnight accommodations in otherwise unfamiliar vacation territory. By the mid-1950s, there were more than four hundred HoJo's restaurants nationwide, and the company's market dominance lasted into the early 1960s, when national fast-food chains—ironically, a marketing concept that Howard Johnson had originally pioneered—began to cut into the Howard Johnson market.

Beginning in 1980, when the original Howard Johnson's son sold the chain (the senior Johnson retired in 1959 and died in 1972), it suffered a surprisingly rapid decline, as successive corporate owners mismanaged the company and couldn't decide which aspects of it they wanted to retain—the motels or the traditional restaurant business. Lawsuits over trademark dishes by franchisees fleeing the corporate ownership further complicated the business and hastened its demise.

The Asbury Park Howard Johnson's, which opened in 1962 at the height of the chain's reputation, occupied a new boardwalk restaurant building constructed as part of a modernistic pavilion, which included a rooftop band shell. The pavilion was commissioned by the City of Asbury Park, which owned the boardwalk, and designed by Philadelphia architect John Fridy to replace the old run-down Fifth Avenue Arcade. When it opened, the restaurant displayed the characteristic orange and blue Howard Johnson's

The former Howard Johnson's, now Tim McLoone's restaurant, in 2012. *Courtesy of the Asbury Park Library.*

color scheme that informed and comforted travelers from afar nationwide. The familiar family restaurant was located on the boardwalk level, but a second-floor "Panorama Room" housed a separate restaurant and cocktail lounge—not a usual feature of the chain's restaurants. Interestingly, the upstairs aspect of the lounge made it compliant with Asbury Park founder James A. Bradley's longtime prohibition of alcohol sales on the boardwalk, which endured even after the rest of the city went "wet." The restaurant's proximity to Convention Hall seemed to guarantee a steady stream of year-round business forever.

The Asbury Park Howard Johnson's thrived through the 1960s, crowded with patrons from nearby Convention Hall events, tourists who walked over from the nearby Berkeley-Carteret hotel and day-trip beachgoers. Lines of customers waiting for a chance to down

The former Howard Johnson's, now Tim McLoone's restaurant as seen from the boardwalk in 2012. McLoone added an outside dining feature. *Courtesy of Joseph Bilby.*

HoJo standards like fried clams, hot dogs in New England–style rolls and, of course, the delightful twenty-eight ice cream flavors often wound down the boardwalk, frequently serenaded by tunes from a band in the pavilion's rooftop venue. In the 1970s, however, business began to decline, and by the 1980s, it had slipped into an ever more rapid downward spiral. As the chain declined nationally, so did its Asbury Park boardwalk location. With the closure of the Woodbridge Howard Johnson's in 1998, the Asbury Park restaurant became the last HoJo in New Jersey—and one of only five extant in the whole country.

Over the years of decline, franchise owner George Panas reduced his staff—which numbered eighty people at one high point—restricted the restaurant's open hours, condensed his menu to one page and even took in items like broken watches in trade for meals from, as one press report characterized it, an "increasingly indigent clientele." In the end, the restaurant was open but a few hours a day, depending on the occasional private party or Bruce Springsteen appearance in town for any income at all. In an effort to keep some semblance of the good old days alive on the boardwalk, the city reduced Panas's lease payments. In June 2006, he finally gave up, selling his liquor license (a valuable commodity in New Jersey) for $250,000 to Asbury Partners, a corporation contracted by the city to rebuild the city's oceanfront that had purchased all the Asbury Park boardwalk pavilions.

Panas, by then seventy-six, had had enough and retired, but he had faith that his old building would survive and make a comeback as a restaurant venue in a better tomorrow. His assumption proved correct. The old Howard Johnson's was reopened in 2008 by New Jersey Shore musician and restaurateur Tim McLoone, who owns a number of dining establishments at other locations from West Orange, New Jersey, to Maryland. McLoone reopened the upstairs lounge as Tim McLoone's Supper Club, where patrons can order drinks with their meals and enjoy performances by musicians and comedians on weekend nights. The lower level became McLoone's Asbury Grille, with seating both inside and out on the boardwalk. While he reconstructed the old building's badly decaying interior, McLoone restored the external look of the old Asbury Park HoJo's so that if they drove by, Don and Megan Draper, along with nostalgic 1960s kids, would have no trouble spotting a familiar food stop on the road.

THE STONE PONY

913 Ocean Avenue

732-502-0600

stoneponyonline.com/index.html

GPS: 40° 13' 11.92" N, 74° 00' 02.59" W

Music aficionados worldwide are familiar with Asbury Park's Stone Pony, but few know the back story of the site. Although not many remember it today, it all sort of started with John and Ida Jacobs back in 1922, when they opened Mrs. Jay's at the corner of Second and Ocean Avenues in Asbury Park, selling hot dogs that old-timers—locals as well as tourists—recollect with a particularly vibrant nostalgia. Neptune native Bob Pontecorvo recalls that when his mother got a craving for a Mrs. Jay's hot dog back in the 1950s, there was no stopping her. Mrs. Pontecorvo did not drive, so she would make her son—who had just been discharged from the army and was living at home while he went to college—chauffer her over to Asbury Park for a dog and a brew in Mrs. Jay's open-air beer garden, where ocean breezes wafted in from the nearby surf and cooled the patrons on a hot summer's day.

If Mrs. Jay's had a classic epoch, it was indeed the 1950s, as Asbury Park, moving beyond the dismal days and the horrors of the Depression and World War II, was entering one of its periodic comeback eras. Although John and Ida started out by leasing a hot dog concession in 1922, they expanded it early on by buying the building and lot and turning it into Mrs. Jay's Restaurant, with an adjacent beer garden serving 2 percent beer. In the early 1930s, in the happy wake of the end of Prohibition, the restaurant began selling hard liquor at the restaurant's Circus Bar and real beer in the outdoor beer garden, also offering occasional musical

The Stone Pony, one of the most iconic rock-and-roll music venues in the United States, still stands. *Courtesy of Joseph Bilby.*

performances, starting a tradition of entertainment on the site that would come to full fruition decades later.

Ida, the original Mrs. Jay, died in 1939, and her husband, John, passed away the following year. Although the Jacobs were gone by 1940, Mrs. Jay's lived on under the auspices of daughter Jeanette and son-in-law Murray Weiner. In the 1960s, a customer could consult a palm reader while sipping a beer in the garden and, by 1965, watch go-go girls dance on a stage. The family eventually sold the restaurant building, which briefly became a disco dance club known as the Magic Touch, while continuing to operate the beer garden, which became well known as a biker hangout in the 1970s and 1980s, best remembered for a police bust when a go-go girl (or, in some accounts, a waitress) performed in a transparent blouse wearing no brassiere. Eventually, the beer garden closed during the overall downward slump of Asbury Park in the 1980s.

On February 8, 1974, following the demise of the disco club, entrepreneurial rock music aficionados Jack Roig and Butch Pielka purchased the old Mrs. Jay's restaurant building. The new owners reopened the site as a nightclub and music venue they dubbed the Stone Pony, a name Pielka recalled that he had conjured up in a dream, and a legend was born. At the time, however, there was no way to predict that eventual legendary status, and initial indications were far from promising. There was a snowstorm on opening night, the heating failed and gross receipts totaled one dollar. The Stone Pony stayed open, however, struggling through to the end of the year, bringing in musical acts that Pielka knew from working at the Riptide, a Point Pleasant club, but did not seem to catch on in Asbury Park. The city fathers were not helpful, as they didn't want another rock-and-roll venue in town.

It seemed that the adventure was over for the partners when the bill collectors were beating on the door that December, but the club's first house band, the Blackberry Booze Band, began to play that month and instantly attracted a large and ultimately profitable audience. The band, featuring local talents "Southside Johnny" Lyon of Ocean Grove and Steve Van Zandt of Middletown, evolved into the renowned Southside Johnny and the Asbury Jukes. The Jukes played at the club three nights a week, and their first album, cut in 1976, was promoted by a live concert broadcast via radio from the Stone Pony.

The 1970s and 1980s saw an explosion of music at the now hot club, with bands playing to a packed house in a wide variety of music styles, including dance tunes and classic, country and hard rock, as well as reggae. Asbury Park began to sink in the 1980s, but the Stone Pony continued to rise. As the club became a renowned and nationally respected venue, it began to showcase well-known performers and groups. The Stone Pony hosted Elvis Costello, the Ramones, Stevie Ray Vaughn and Blondie, among many others, and "the Pony," as it became known in the vernacular, also provided a welcome venue for charitable and benefit concerts. As an extra bonus, Bruce Springsteen and members of his E Street Band, including Clarence Clemons, often showed up at the club for impromptu gigs between tours. The Stone Pony, it appeared to all who came to hear the music, had made it.

Fame is often not enough, however, and by the late 1980s, the Stone Pony, along with a number of other live music clubs in New Jersey and elsewhere, ran into economic difficulties, including those caused by rapidly rising insurance rates. Although a group of employees attempted to buy the fiscally troubled club in 1991, Roig and Pielka filed for bankruptcy, and the Stone Pony was purchased by Steven Nasar of neighboring Deal, New Jersey. Nasar appreciated the Pony's heritage and continued to schedule nationally known music acts through 1998 but then decided to close the Stone Pony and turn it into Vinyl, a dance club. There was one last weekend of performances, however, dubbed the "Pony's Last Ride." The extended show featured a surprise appearance by Southside Johnny. And then, it seemed, the Pony was dead—but not for long.

As the twentieth century came to a close, Asbury Park was poised for yet another comeback, and Cuban American restaurateur Domenic Santana of Jersey City was visiting the city when a friend pointed out the then-former Stone Pony and noted its place in rock-and-roll history. Impressed, Santana rounded up some other investors and bought the club in February 2000, planning to reopen it under the old name. By this time, it was widely realized, by Santana and others, that the Stone Pony was much more than just a popular rock-and-roll venue. It was an iconic bit of New Jerseyana that had, in its previous decades, garnered a fame that extended far beyond its city, state and even nation. Santana and his partners gave the old building a "slick nostalgic makeover," and the Stone Pony was reopened and rededicated in May 2000. New Jersey governor Christine Todd Whitman gave the rededication keynote address and, without exaggeration, declared that the club's importance was "not just to us, but to the world."

Santana sold the club in 2003, but as the twenty-first century moves along, the Pony prances on as a major music venue, once again the site of dynamic performances, numerous charity fundraisers and, in 2004, the first location for the Bamboozle rock festival, sited on the location of the old Mrs. Jay's beer garden. Bamboozle outgrew the Stone Pony and moved around the country, returning to Asbury Park, where it was held on the beach, in 2012.

Never content to rest on its ample laurels, the Stone Pony has upgraded its sound, lighting and air conditioning and installed a new roof in 2009—a good thing, as collapsing roofs have been responsible for the ultimate demolition of a number of Asbury Park historic sites, including the Baronet Theater. Refitted and ready for the next generation, there is no doubt the legendary rock club by the sea will be around for a very long time to come.

BARONET THEATER (DEMOLISHED)

205 Fourth Avenue
www.youtube.com/watch?v=_PQSUEvt_vk
GPS: 40° 13' 22.65" N, 73° 59' 59.35" W

On September 25, 2010, they razed the Baronet. After ninety-seven years, the iconic Asbury Park theater was no more. Although there had been hope that it would end otherwise, the Baronet had met the fate of its far flashier relatives, the Saint James, the Lyric and the Mayfair—crumbled into the trash bin of the city by the sea. It was a sad moment for the members of the Asbury Park Historical Society, who realized the old building's significance and importance to their city's story, as well as for the members of the general public who had patronized the theater over the years and remembered it fondly.

The 546-seat Baronet, located on the corner of Kingsley and Fourth Avenues, opened its doors as the Ocean Theater in 1913. The new theater was intended to be primarily a vaudeville venue but would also show films, a dual-use tradition that continued into the 1930s. Although a recent reporter classified the place as "one step above a nickelodeon," it was far more than that. A host of well-known stage acts of the era appeared at the Ocean, including, according to one report, the Three Stooges.

The Ocean was purchased by Asbury Park–based impresario Walter Reade Jr. in 1953, shortly after the death of his father, who had founded the Reade theater empire that spanned several

Asbury Lanes, a bowling alley and music venue that has survived the reconstruction of much of the town relatively intact. *Courtesy of Joseph Bilby*.

states. The Ocean joined other local theaters, including Asbury Park's classy Mayfair, Saint James, Lyric, Savoy and Paramount theaters, the latter built as part of the Convention Hall complex, in the Reade chain. Reade renamed his new acquisition the Baronet, using a spare marquee from one of his New York City properties to announce the change.

Unfortunately for the Baronet, the Reade theater empire began to crumble with the growth of suburban drive-ins and then multiplex theaters in the post–World War II years, a process that accelerated in the 1970s. Although the drive-in phenomenon did not endure, the suburban theater was here to stay. Reade died in a Swiss skiing accident in 1973. His corporate successors, realizing that the fancy Mayfair and Saint James, palatial Reade houses dating from the golden age of Hollywood films, were far too expensive to maintain in the new era, committed both to the wrecking ball in the 1970s. The much less ostentatious Baronet soldiered on to the end of the century but under new ownership.

Over its long life, the film genres that flickered on the Baronet's screen changed with the times. In the late 1960s, the theater was showing artsy foreign motion pictures, and author Joseph G. Bilby recalls seeing the depressing Swedish film *Elvira Madigan* there with his future wife after his return from Vietnam in 1967. In the 1970s, the Baronet switched to lighter fare, with Disney-style family entertainment. In 1975, local-boy-made-good Danny DeVito used the theater for a special family and friends showing of his film *Minestrone*. As Asbury Park began its rapid downhill slide in the 1980s, however, the Baronet switched to showing triple X–rated movies.

The Baronet changed ownership and opened and closed intermittently in its final decades. In December 2005, Dennis Dubrow and Patrick Fasano, the latter a longtime Asbury Park area developer, bought the theater, along with the adjacent Fast

Lane music club, one of the city's famous rock-and-roll venues. The Fast Lane had hosted performances by U2 and Bruce Springsteen and was where a young Jon Bon Jovi got his start in the business. The partners tried to make a go of the Baronet, their confidence based on the early twenty-first-century signs of revival in Asbury Park. They made extensive renovations on and restorations to the aging building, which reopened in the summer of 2006 as a "$2 movie house," which, to the delight of history buffs, used "the vintage 1933 carbon-arc projectors" to show those movies. Dubrow told a *New York Times* reporter at the time that he and Fasano had "saved a little bit of Asbury Park's history here. What's going to happen now, I don't know."

Admittedly, the future did not look good. The Asbury Park City Council, determined to assist Asbury Partners, the corporation to which it had turned over the oceanfront in hopes of establishing a condo metropolis, threatened to condemn and seize the theater using eminent domain and turn it over to its corporate partners. There was a good deal of friction between the Baronet's owners and the city, with city officials accusing Dubrow and Fasano of buying the theater and club just to resell them at a higher price, which, considering their investments of time and money, did not seem likely.

The Baronet survived in private hands through 2007, when the partners finally sold it to Asbury Partners, which, in turn, passed it on to the successor company iStar Financial. The theater stood unused until it was declared "structurally unsound" in 2010 and subsequently demolished. There would be no condos springing up, though, and as of the summer of 2012, the Baronet site remained a vacant lot, with the shuttered Fast Lane, ironically, still standing and Asbury Lanes, a bowling alley that doubles as a music venue, the only operating business on the block.

The site of the Baronet, now a vacant lot. *Courtesy of Joseph Bilby*.

Prior to its demolition, the wrecking crew salvaged some priceless artifacts from the Baronet, including Reade's old marquee, reels of film, printed material, a mural, chandeliers and several of those priceless old projectors. The artifacts were safely stored, and Asbury Park Historical Society president Don Stine is hopeful that they can be properly displayed as relics of Asbury's fascinating past at some future date.

Local historian Gary Crawford, who had run a projector in the Baronet back in the 1970s, remarked to a *Newark Star Ledger* reporter that he felt bad when the theater building was destroyed. "It was like an old friend," he continued. "But then you can't save everything. I understand that."

ASBURY PARK LIBRARY

501 First Avenue (Corner of First and Grand Avenues)

732-774-4221

asburyparklibrary.org

GPS: 40° 13' 13.40" N, 74° 00' 26.56" W

The Asbury Park Library traces its origins to the Asbury Park and Ocean Grove Library Association, which was founded on November 23, 1878. The association grew out of an earlier informal literary club founded by Helen M. Bradley, wife of the city's founding father, James A. Bradley. The present library still owns and displays a marble block—perhaps intended to be used in conjunction with a gavel during meetings—engraved with the institution's founding date.

In 1881, Mr. Bradley deeded two lots at the corner of First and Grand Avenues to the Library Association as a site for a library building. He subsequently hired a New York City architect to formally design the structure, and construction work—contracted for with a Bridgeport, Connecticut company for $16,000—began in 1882. As was his wont, the Founder, no doubt in one of his "up" phases, tended toward the grandiose and envisioned the building as including a museum and auditorium. Although it never housed a formal auditorium, the library main floor originally had a stage for musical events and perhaps drama productions, and a ticket window for admissions collection is still present in the entrance hall. The proposed museum apparently never amounted to much, and its contents went missing over the years.

The construction project dragged on for some time and was still not finished when the library formally opened in 1885. Construction was not totally completed until the late 1890s. The library building design was inspired by the then–cutting edge Queen Anne or

English Baroque school of architecture that became quite popular in post–Civil War America. Although the style was intended to evoke designs common during the 1702–14 reign of Queen Anne of England, late nineteenth- and early twentieth-century American Queen Anne buildings actually bear little resemblance to their early eighteenth-century forebears.

American Queen Anne buildings are actually better classified by the alternate English Baroque characterization and feature wraparound porches and an assortment of decorative towers, prominent chimneys and gables, achieving a "gingerbread" look often generically called Victorian by modern real estate brokers. One distinctive Queen Anne feature of the library was a typical tall tower on the building's northeast corner. In 1930, during the administration of Asbury Park mayor Clarence Hetrick, the library was "modernized" by the removal of the tower and its adjacent chimney and gable.

The Asbury Park Library in the early twentieth century, when it still boasted its unique Queen Anne tower. *Courtesy of the Asbury Park Library.*

The Asbury Park Library in the 1950s, shorn of its tower and chimney. The stained glass window dedicated to Ulysses S. Grant can be seen to the rear. *Courtesy of the Asbury Park Library.*

The Asbury Park Library in 2012. *Courtesy of Joseph Bilby.*

The late nineteenth-century Asbury Park Library, was, present librarian Robert Stewart explains, a "private subscription library," which meant that in order to be a member one had to "join the association and pay dues." The library was under the direct control of the Library Association Board, of which Mr. and Mrs. Bradley were influential members. An 1897 referendum, passed by a slim majority of Asbury Park voters, established a public library, and management of the Bradley-era library, as well as ownership of the property and building, was formally transferred to the city. An appointed board of trustees assumed operation of the library in trust for the citizens of Asbury Park. In a subsequent referendum, the voters approved a bond issue to assume Bradley's remaining mortgage (there were rumors of foreclosure) and complete construction of the library building itself. On his death in 1921, Bradley left the library a legacy of $6,812.

Today, the Asbury Park Library holds over 100,000 volumes, a significant microfilm collection and an archive of newspaper clippings, documents and images relating to the city's history. It serves thousands of registered patrons inside and out of Asbury Park and is an indispensible stop for anyone doing research on the history of the city.

Two stained-glass library windows provide major artistic attractions within the building. The memorial window on the east side of the library is dedicated to Civil War hero and President Ulysses S. Grant, who owned property and spent his summers in nearby Long Branch. Following Grant's death on July 25, 1885, a friend of the former chief executive—noted Philadelphia newspaper publisher, real estate developer and philanthropist George W. Childs—contracted with Alfred Godwin and Company to design and craft the window and install it as a memorial tribute to the late president. The window was dedicated in March 1886 in a ceremony organized by the

Caldwell K. Hall Grand Army of the Republic Post, an Asbury Park Civil War veterans' organization. James A. Bradley spoke on the occasion, and letters from a number of notables, including Major Generals William T. Sherman and Philip Sheridan, were read. The former president's widow visited the library that August to view the memorial.

The window design on the western side of the building is traditionally attributed to Asbury Park artist Theodore H. Davis, although no firm documentation exists. The design was apparently inspired by poet Henry Wadsworth Longfellow's 1849 poem "Tegner's Drapa [death song or dirge]," an allusion to an ancient

The Ulysses S. Grant stained-glass window in the Asbury Park Library. *Courtesy of Joseph Bilby.*

The Asbury Park Library's second stained-glass window, designed by a local artist on a theme inspired by a Henry Wadsworth Longfellow poem on an ancient Norse myth. *Courtesy of Joseph Bilby.*

Norse saga, which appeared in his larger work "The Seaside and the Fireside," although a number of Longfellow's other titles are noted on the perimeter of the design. Librarian Stewart noted that "Longfellow was immensely popular at the time and had a kind of 'rock star' status."

The window, crafted by the renowned Tiffany Company, portrays the designer's interpretation of the sea burial of the Viking deity Balder the Beautiful, as described in the poem. Other than that it was probably in the late nineteenth century, it is unclear when the window was installed or, for that matter, who presented it to the library. An authoritative book on Tiffany windows calls it the "Mitchell Memorial Window." Dr. Henry Mitchell was a prominent Asbury Park physician and member of the library board of trustees. Some accounts state variously that it was a gift of "the people of Asbury Park" or "the women of Asbury Park," perhaps in honor of Dr. Mitchell.

With its stunning stained-glass windows, and its invaluable books and archives, the Asbury Park library is a must-see stop on any tour of the city's historic sites.

Tour 2

DOWNTOWN

STEINBACH'S DEPARTMENT STORE, NOW OLD MAN RAFFERTY'S

541 Cookman Avenue
www.oldmanraffertys.com
GPS: 40° 12' 58.43" N, 74° 00' 36.12" W

For decades, the tall, stately Steinbach building dominated downtown Asbury Park, reigning as a powerful symbol of the city's status as the premier shopping destination for thousands of consumers throughout Monmouth County and beyond. Steinbach's was perhaps the most glamorous and comprehensive department store for miles around, its five stories stocked with everything from the latest fashions to the finest in furniture. For those important retail purchases, everyone in the hinterlands and down the coast went to Asbury Park, and for most of the twentieth century, the imposing Steinbach's was the hub of shopping activity in the city center. Well-heeled customers crowded the aisles and counters, grabbed a quick bite in the store's luncheonette and headed home by car or on the fleet of buses that regularly stopped in front of the building's enormous plate-glass windows fronting on Cookman Avenue.

Well into the 1960s, Steinbach's remained the place to shop on the north Jersey coast. Judy Feinstein, who now works in one of the trendy specialty shops that line Cookman Avenue, recalled that a trip to the legendary department store during that era was an event. "You dressed yourself and your children up to come downtown," she said. "And Steinbach's was the highlight of a trip to Asbury. That's where you bought your clothes, gifts for special occasions—everything."

The opulent cornerstone of Asbury Park commerce began as a small storefront during the city's early years, when James A. Bradley's shore settlement, carved out of sand dunes and brush, resembled a frontier town. During the late 1870s, when the store was at the corner of Lake Avenue and Main Street, it was a simple enterprise with goods heaped on a counter, overseen by a single clerk in a gas-lit room. But as Asbury Park grew, so did the ambitions of John Steinbach, the store's founder.

In the 1890s, Steinbach embarked on a massive construction project that resulted in the new store on Cookman Avenue. He hired New York building designers Robert Cleverdon and Joseph Putzel to create his shrine to shopping, and the pair chose a brick and Italianate style popular among merchants at the time. With its eye-catching plate-glass windows, beige brick exterior and sumptuous interior of mahogany staircases and terra cotta molding, the magnificent structure was designed to represent the rising social status of Asbury Park. Although it was originally built as a four-story structure, a fifth floor was added several years later to make the building even more imposing.

In 1906, the *Asbury Journal* singled out the Steinbach building as an impressive example of architectural genius and heaped praise

Steinbach's Department Store as it appeared in the early twentieth century. *Courtesy of the Asbury Park Library.*

upon its designers. The article provided a detailed tour of the store, starting with descriptions of the impressive counters and showcases on the first floor and then moving on to the second level, which was devoted to men's and women's clothing. The third floor featured crockery and had a separate department for hardware, "where one can buy any article entering into the construction of a house." The next two floors, occupying a space of nearly thirty thousand square feet, featured "furniture of every description modeled after the colonial, mission and Louis XVI styles."

The writer was especially lavish in his praise of the fifth floor, with its richly stained wood trim and Chinese-white walls. One of the principal features of the room was a large imitation fireplace on the south wall with a finish of weathered oak. "The Steinbach Company has set a pace for others to follow, and while it would be impossible for all to build a 'Mammoth,' yet the

Steinbach's Department Store, circa 1960. It was still "the place to shop" in Monmouth County. *Courtesy of the Asbury Park Library.*

generous treatment of their building in all its entirety should be an example for others, however small their undertaking," the reporter gushed.

To establish and maintain such a business required stamina and vision, and John Steinbach represented the type of feisty, single-minded entrepreneur who molded Asbury Park into a formidable business hub. He moved to the United States from Austria via Halifax, Canada, and opened his first store in Long Branch. Seeing the potential for expansion, he summoned his brothers, Henry and Jacob, from Europe and began to consolidate his department store mini-empire. John Steinbach believed in personalized service and would greet each of his customers, making sure no one was waiting for service. His wife, Eugenia, had two children, Walter and Arthur, but died shortly after Walter's birth. The grief-stricken Steinbach never remarried.

Instead, the elder Steinbach threw himself into the business, leaving the care of his sons to the family "help," supervised by his housekeeper. As the two boys grew into manhood, Walter became a philanthropist who was devoted to the needy, while Arthur evolved into a rigid businessman. Both men remained involved in the family business, embarking on annual buying expeditions to Europe to find the latest designs in Bavarian china, Irish linen, Parisian hats and other novelties to line the store's shelves and counters.

By the early twentieth century, Steinbach's was recognized as the epitome of upscale one-stop shopping in the shore area. Even

The Steinbach building today. The first floor is home to Old Man Rafferty's restaurant, a gelato shop and other businesses. The upper floors have been made into condominium apartments. *Courtesy of Joseph Bilby.*

in the depths of the Depression, the store boasted a full-page ad in an edition of 1937's *Monmouth Pictorial,* a high-end magazine that covered the comings and goings of local society, from dinner dances in Rumson to house parties in Middletown. Characterizing Steinbach's as "the world's largest department store," the ad boasted that the store "offers the public all that any metropolitan department store can offer plus the convenience of home shopping in a big store, which through its employees and business policy has never lost the personal touch."

Steinbach's regional superstore reign endured into the 1960s, but at the end of that decade, the lure of shopping malls and hints of the coming decline of Asbury Park as a summer resort, as well as racial riots in 1970 that accelerated the flight of residents and merchants from the city, began to erode a once-loyal customer base. Steinbach's cash registers rang for the last time in 1979, when its doors were permanently shut on a grim Saturday in July. The business name survived for several years in some suburban mall stores, but those locations eventually suffered the same fate as the original Steinbach's.

For years, the shuttered Asbury Park store stood as a depressing reminder of the city's deterioration, but in 2007, New York developer Carter Sackman opened the renovated building for business, preserving its historic exterior architectural details while creating twenty-two thousand square feet of retail space on the first floor and sixty-three lofts, apartments and penthouses on three upper floors (the original fifth floor was destroyed in a 1989 fire).

The popular restaurant Old Man Rafferty's now anchors the building, and patrons dine at outside tables sheltered by red umbrellas on warm summer evenings. Other businesses include a sleek sports bar and a gelato shop, and on weekend nights, the former Steinbach's is a hub of activity. Once again, the grand old department store presides over a bustling downtown as a symbol of Asbury Park's enduring energy and allure.

The Byram Building, aka Post Office Building, now Fish Restaurant

601 Mattison Avenue

www.fishasburypark.com

www.criticalpast.com/video/65675045971_President-Woodrow-Wilson_ Asbury-Park_coming-out-of-building_people-gather

GPS: 40° 12' 58.48" N, 74° 00' 37.39" W

Most people are aware that Woodrow Wilson served two terms as president of the United States. Fewer realize that he was governor of New Jersey at the time of his first presidential election and fewer still that in the summer and early autumn of 1916, he visited Asbury Park often and even maintained a large office in the city on the fifth floor of the Byram building.

The Virginia-born Wilson was a professor at Princeton University before being elected president of the university in 1902. Having established a reputation as a reformer, he was persuaded to accept the New Jersey Democratic nomination for governor and successfully ran for that office in 1910. By 1912, he was a leading contender for the Democratic presidential nomination, which he won in June of that year. A large delegation of national Democratic politicians traveled to the New Jersey governor's summer home in Sea Girt to congratulate him.

There were three candidates in the presidential election of 1912, with Republican William Howard Taft running for a second term and former Republican president Theodore Roosevelt, who was dissatisfied with the Taft administration, running on the

A late nineteenth-century view of downtown Asbury Park, at the junction of Cookman and Mattison Avenues, with the Byram building, then the site of the city post office, on the right. *Courtesy of the Asbury Park Library.*

independent Bull Moose Party ticket. Wilson won only 43 percent of the popular vote that year but managed to take the majority of the Electoral College votes and so was elected president of the United States.

In 1916, with World War I raging in Europe, Wilson ran for a second term, using the campaign slogan "He kept us out of war," even though it appeared that eventual American entry into the conflict was almost inevitable. That summer, Wilson established his "Summer White House" home at the Shadow Lawn estate of his supporter Joseph Benedict Greenhut in West Long Branch, and his campaign staff established its headquarters on the fifth floor of the Byram building in Asbury Park. Wilson won reelection against Republican candidate Charles Evans Hughes, taking the Electoral College vote once again but failing once more to win the popular vote. The United States formally declared war on Germany on April 6, 1917. (To view a brief video clip of President Wilson and

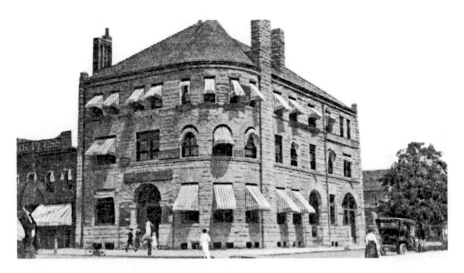

The Byram building and the *Asbury Park Press* buildings stood side by side in the early twentieth century. In modified form, they still do. The upper floors of the Byram building were leased for professional offices. *Courtesy of the Asbury Park Library.*

his wife leaving the Byram building in 1916, see the link posted at the beginning of this section.)

President Wilson was not unfamiliar with Asbury Park. As governor of New Jersey, he had vacationed at the state's summer capital, the New Jersey National Guard training ground at Sea Girt, a few miles down the coast. In August 1911, he visited the city twice, initially to address the Association of Municipal and County Clerks meeting at the Brunswick Hotel and returning a week later with his military staff as guests of "Queen Titania," who presided over the resort city's annual Baby Parade.

The office building occupied by the Wilson campaign headquarters in 1916 was perhaps the most solid-appearing building in Asbury Park. It was originally built in 1885 in the Richardsonian Romanesque style to house, appropriately enough, a financial institution, the Asbury Park National Bank and Trust Company. The building's style, a variation on the popular

By the summer of 1916, the Byram building had added two stories and was taken over by a bank, Asbury Park Trust Company. President Woodrow Wilson's reelection campaign leased the fifth floor in the summer and fall of 1916. *Courtesy of Don Stine.*

nineteenth-century Romanesque Revival movement inspired by eleventh- and twelfth-century French architecture, was named after prominent Louisiana-born Massachusetts architect Henry Hobson Richardson, who studied at both Harvard and the École des Beaux-Arts in Paris and was its best-known American practitioner.

In 1895, the United States Post Office moved into the first floor of what was then the three-story Romanesque-style Byram building, with its upstairs floors' office space in use by a range of professionals and businesses from attorneys and dentists to the editorial offices of local promotional magazines like *Seashore Life* and *Seaside Torch*, as well as the *New York Times* and *Brooklyn Eagle* newspapers. In the late nineteenth and early twentieth centuries, the *New York Times* and other large metropolitan dailies devoted heavy coverage to New Jersey affairs and especially to the most popular Jersey Shore resort areas in the summertime.

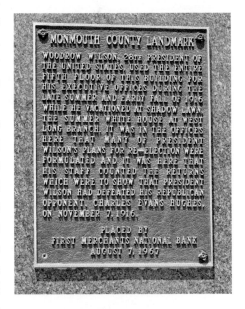

Early in 1916, following the disastrous fire that destroyed the wooden-frame *Asbury Park Press* building next door and collapsed the Byram building's roof, two more stories were tacked on to the structure in a seamless addition that preserved the original construction design style. By then it was the home of the First Merchants National Bank, which occupied the

A historical marker plaque commemorating its use by the Wilson campaign was installed on the Byram building, then the headquarters of the First Merchants National Bank, in 1967. *Courtesy of the Asbury Park Library.*

ground floor when the Wilson campaign leased the top floor. In 1967, First Merchants mounted a plaque on the outside wall of the building commemorating President Wilson's use of the fifth-floor office space in 1916. Perhaps surprisingly, considering the bad times the city endured before its revival, the plaque remains intact to this day.

As Asbury Park began its downward spiral in the 1980s, the Byram building was abandoned and had reached its nadir when restaurateurs Jim and Karen DeGilio, after eighteen months of renovations—including removing bricks that concealed the once stylish arched windows—opened their spacious 5,500-square-foot, 154-seat seafood restaurant, Fish, on the first floor in October 2010. The floors above the highly regarded restaurant have been converted into luxury condominium apartments, completing the revival of this splendid old building.

ASBURY PARK PRESS BUILDING

603 Mattison Avenue

www.app.com

GPS: 40° 12' 58.66" N, 74° 00' 38.29" W

The stately five-story *Asbury Park Press* building represents an era when print journalism was king and brash newsboys hawked the day's events on bustling street corners. For many decades after its founding in 1879, the *Asbury Park Press*, originally known as the *Shore Press*, was truly the voice and "paper of record" for Monmouth and Ocean Counties, and its imposing headquarters at 603 Mattison Avenue was designed to represent the newspaper's importance and influence.

The *Asbury Park Press* building, a five-story structure built to replace the original three-story wood-frame building, which was destroyed by fire in January 1916. It was headquarters for the newspaper until it moved to Neptune Township in the 1980s. *Courtesy of Joseph Bilby.*

It was an overwhelming calamity, however, that inspired the building's construction. The *Press* was previously housed in a three-story frame building at the same location, but a devastating fire consumed the operation on January 17, 1916. The blaze erupted about 4:30 a.m., and the flames' reflection awakened Thomas Winckler, whose Bangs Avenue house was behind the building. Winckler sent his stable man to sound a nearby alarm box, and within minutes, firefighters were struggling to keep the blaze from consuming not only the *Press* headquarters but also the adjacent Byram building, home of the Asbury Park Trust Company and today the location of Fish restaurant. The fire quickly turned the *Press* building into a roaring furnace and destroyed everything except the large printing press on the first floor, while the Byram building suffered a collapsed roof.

Faced with such a catastrophe, the *Press*'s owner and editor, respected local businessman J. Lyle Kinmonth, made it his first priority to ensure that publication of the daily newspaper would continue. Newsmen set up an operation in a house on Bangs Avenue, and the paper was temporarily printed at a facility in Long Branch. More importantly, Kinmonth resolved to build a bigger, more prestigious home for the *Press*, and the new, five-story concrete and brick building was in operation that same year.

Certainly Kinmonth was the type of goal-oriented, intelligent entrepreneur who would guarantee a quick and effective response to adversity. He was described as a "true type of the progressive, well-balanced 20th century businessman" in a 1920s history of Monmouth County. Born near Columbus City, Iowa, in 1870, he received a bachelor's degree in philosophy from the University of Iowa and undertook postgraduate courses in Philadelphia at the University of Pennsylvania before arriving in Asbury Park to take control of the *Press* from his uncle and the newspaper's founder, Dr. Hugh S. Kinmonth. The younger Kinmonth "quickly familiarized himself with every department of the newspaper establishment," according to the Monmouth County historic guide, and moved the publication forward with numerous innovations, including changing the paper from a weekly to a daily product and adding a Sunday edition.

After the 1916 fire struck its devastating blow to *Press* operations, Kinmonth moved quickly to build his new headquarters. The structure was an impressive one, befitting the newspaper's importance as the voice of Asbury Park and its "suburbs." The exterior was decorated with patterned brick, mullioned windows and a row of concrete lions' heads placed above the fifth-floor windows. The paper's loading docks were on the opposite side of the building, which fronted on Bangs Avenue.

Behind the handsome façade, however, was a hard-driving news operation that raced to satisfy a voracious readership hungry

The Tusting Piano Company was right next door to the new *Asbury Park Press* building erected in 1916. This photo was taken in the 1920s. *Courtesy of the Asbury Park Library.*

for the latest local, national and international news. Kinmonth was committed to ensuring that the *Asbury Park Press* kept its competitive edge and was willing to spend considerable sums of money to do so. A 1921 *Press* article boasted of the newsroom's newest addition, a teletype printer that allowed Associated Press news stories to be sent over the wire via Western Union. "The printer works all day, from 7 o'clock in the morning until evening, with a break of a few minutes for lunch," the article noted, adding that the quantity of news was "enormous" and printed out at sixty-five words a minute. Purchasing the expensive, state-of-the-art teletype was an example of Kinmonth's commitment to keep the *Press* ahead of its competition by "enlarging its facilities and extending its scope," according to a 1920s profile.

Under Kinmonth's direction, the *Press* continued to grow and prosper. Following his death in 1945, Kinmonth's chosen successors, senior executives Wayne D. McMurray and Ernest W. Lass, carried on the legacy of innovation and expansion. Recognizing the enormous popularity of radio, the new owners invested in their own station, WJLK, named after Kinmonth. The studio operated from *Press* headquarters, and its 1:00 p.m. newscast was the station's most-listened-to program because it included a reading of the daily obituaries from the pages of the *Press*.

In the 1950s, another developing sociological phenomenon created an enormous opportunity for the newspaper. Returning World War II veterans with growing families and GI Bill mortgage approvals in hand were eager to move out of cities in search of the pleasures of semirural life, and construction of the Garden State Parkway opened up the farmlands of Monmouth and Ocean Counties to suburban sprawl. Urban dwellers flocked to the ranch homes and Cape Cods that began to dot the shore, and the explosive development was a goldmine for the *Press*. The paper's circulation rocketed from 27,000 in 1956 to 127,000 daily and 177,000 on Sunday in 1983.

Capitalizing on such an opportunity required the same decisive leadership exerted by J. Lyle Kinmonth during the paper's early days. Successors McMurray and Lass continued to grow the operation, and their successors, Jules Plangere and Don Lass, Ernest's son, carried on the tradition of innovation and expansion. During their tenure, the *Press* aggressively expanded its coverage throughout Monmouth and Ocean Counties and began to seriously pursue investigative journalism on a consistent basis. One of Plangere's and Lass's most admirable decisions was to continually reinvest profits into the news operation. "I have never been told that I spent too much on a story," Sunday editor Si Liberman said during an interview in the early 1980s.

Throughout most of the twentieth century, the *Asbury Park Press* building was a significant landmark in downtown Asbury Park, and its reporters, advertising executives and pressmen charged through its glass doors each day prepared to wrestle with the pressures, joys and frustrations of putting out a daily newspaper for a demanding public. Over the years, the stories that filled the paper's pages ranged from the mundane to the momentous. Some of them—such as the Hindenburg explosion, the 1934 *Morro Castle* ship fire disaster and the city's riots of 1970—would be dissected and analyzed for decades afterward. Into the 1970s and early 1980s, the newsroom still crackled with the energy of the classic film *The Front Page*, with chain-smoking reporters hunched over typewriters (computers were just being introduced) while the teletype clacked insistently in the background. *Press* employees were a beloved fixture of the city and provided a much-needed dose of energy at a time when downtown was beginning its long, slow decline.

Thus, it was a shock to many city residents and businessmen when *Press* executives announced their decision to leave Asbury Park for the "suburbs" of Neptune. In 1983, *Press* employees packed their belongings in cardboard boxes and set off for their new home, a gleaming corporate headquarters on a large tract of land off Route 66. When the *Press* building shut its doors for good, the act delivered another massive body blow to the then-deteriorating city of Asbury Park, coming less than ten years after the closure of the massive Steinbach's department store, only steps away around the corner.

The *Press* continued to prosper under the leadership of Plangere and Lass. Like the owners of many other privately owned newspapers, however, they eventually chose to sell the operation to a chain, and in 1997, Gannett purchased the operation. Today, the *Press*, like other newspapers across the country, struggles with the need to adapt to a new consumer society that can choose from a menu of electronic mediums for its daily news. Print journalism is no longer king.

The former *Press* headquarters, meanwhile, has enticed various tenants over the years, ensuring its status as a comparatively well-preserved landmark in downtown Asbury Park. J. Lyle Kinmonth would no doubt be pleased with the creative use of his beloved *Press* building.

THE UPSTAGE

700 Cookman Avenue
www.youtube.com/watch?v=XIznXTAx44A
GPS: 40° 12' 56.17" N, 74° 00' 44.04" W

Today, passersby often refer to it as the "Extreme" building, alluding to the bold red letters that dominate the unassuming storefront on Cookman Avenue and hearken back to its less glamorous days as a shoe store. But more than forty years ago, a steep flight of stairs on the side of that tiny structure led to another world, a windowless room covered in DayGlo images and filled with the sounds of vibrant young musicians who represented a new, fresh and rebellious sound. Known as the Upstage, the narrow space on the third floor became a creative incubator for future giants in the music industry, including "The Boss" himself, Bruce Springsteen.

The iconic rock-and-roll club was the brainchild of hairdressers Tom and Margaret Potter, whose dance parties at their Ocean Grove home proved too much for their more staid and less tolerant neighbors. In 1968, a year of momentous political, social and cultural upheaval, the Potters decided to move their shindigs to the more tolerant community of Asbury Park. After a brief, highly popular stint in a second-floor apartment above Parke Drugstore on Cookman Avenue, the Potters moved the party to the second and third floors of the Thom McCann shoe store on Cookman Avenue and Bond Street and called the club the Upstage.

The second-floor lounge, dubbed the Green Mermaid, was devoted to folk music. Casually dressed waitresses served coffee in little cups while local singers performed cover versions of songs by Joni Mitchell, Joan Baez, Bob Dylan and other singer-songwriters who had upended the fluffy pop fare of the early 1960s with their introspective, soul-searching compositions. The real attraction, however, was on the Upstage's third floor, a windowless, pitch-black room with startling DayGlo wall paintings shimmering under strobe lighting. At midnight, up-and-coming local musicians would form an impromptu house band, and the music would blast until the early morning hours. And while partygoers at more mainstream clubs danced to Top 40 hits, visitors to the Upstate were eager to hear the unexpected—different, eclectic music from passionate young performers.

The Extreme building, on Cookman Avenue, so called because of the Extreme shoe store on its lower level, once hosted the Upstage, a third-floor rock-and-roll venue where a young Bruce Springsteen got his start. *Courtesy of Joseph Bilby.*

In the summer of 1970, the undisputed leader of the Upstage scene was twenty-year-old Bruce Springsteen, who filled the room with his powerful vocals and improvised lyrics. On a typical muggy summer night, the long-haired musician plugged into a standing wall of amplifiers and began an improvised blues song that enraptured the crowd, one musician recalled. Boys with long hair and girls clad in floor-length peasant dresses swayed to the sounds of Springsteen and a host of other talented musicians. It was here, also, that Springsteen met his earliest band mates, drummer Vini Lopez and guitarist Steve Van Zandt.

Despite the venue's popularity, however, the Potters discovered that the business was not a moneymaker. After struggling to keep the Upstage open, the couple admitted defeat in 1971 and closed the club. With only $10,000 left after selling equipment and whatever else they could, they opted to leave New Jersey and head for Florida.

The Upstage, meanwhile, remained shuttered for the next several decades, a darkened time capsule from a creatively charged era, its DayGlo paintings still lining the walls. Throughout the next several decades, as Asbury's downtown lapsed into a state of neglect followed by a slow, stuttering rebirth, the Upstage remained a silent time capsule of the Woodstock era.

It wasn't until 2009, when antiques dealer Richard Yorkowitz purchased the building, that plans began to form for reintroducing the Upstage to a new generation. Yorkowitz harbored a grand vision for the building, wanting to establish a restaurant and event venue on the first two floors and transform the former Upstage into an audio/video production center for musicians and artists. His vision for a "21st century state-of-the-art cultural center and beacon of arts and entertainment" drew widespread support from a cross-section of local artists and businessmen, who rallied to generate public and city support of the plan at the 2010 Asbury Park Planning Board meeting that would determine whether Yorkowitz's idea could move forward. At the jam-packed session, advocates of the proposal, as well as residents with concerns about issues such as excessive noise, all voiced their concerns. After hours of debate, the board agreed to support the necessary ordinance changes to support Yorkowitz's proposal and forwarded the issue to the city council.

Perhaps one of the more poignant moments in the Upstage's recent history was when Bruce Springsteen revisited the site, some forty years after he sang on the club's tiny stage with the intensity of a young man on the verge of success and worldwide fame. As he stood on that stage again and gazed at the murals and graffiti on walls untouched since the club closed decades earlier, Springsteen was overwhelmed with nostalgia.

Yorkowitz, who accompanied him, said Springsteen remarked, "It's a trip!" several times as he surveyed the well-preserved remains of the legendary night spot. The Boss shared some of his memories with Yorkowitz, such as eating at the Green Mermaid Café and earning the princely sum of twenty dollars a night when he was a rising star at the Upstage. Springsteen was also excited about the plans to restore the club, Yorkowitz said.

As city officials continue to mull the zoning changes necessary to restore the Upstage building to its former glory, the site remains an anonymous-looking vacant storefront on a street that is otherwise bustling with activity. Pasted onto its window, as of the summer of 2012, were posters advertising local acts, while the interior has been neatly cleared of debris and filled with pieces of new furniture wrapped in plastic. For now, the Extreme building remains an unassuming structure on busy Cookman Avenue, but its future prospects may establish it as one of the hottest—and most legendary—destinations in town.

ASBURY PARK ARMORY/HAROLD DALEY VFW POST 1333

701 Lake Avenue

732-455-3059

www.facebook.com/pages/Major-Bs-General-Quarters-World-War-II-Scale-
Museum-Gallery/232414630148005

vimeo.com/37265215

GPS: 40° 12' 54.43" N, 74° 00' 46.08" W

The New Jersey National Guard came to Asbury Park in 1906, when Company A of the 3rd New Jersey Infantry was initially headquartered in the city. Company A was subsequently re-designated as Company H of the 3rd. In 1913, the state decided to build a new armory in Asbury Park to serve as a drill hall and weapons and equipment storage facility for the company's soldiers. The site selected was city founder James A. Bradley's old "corporation yard" at the corner of Lake Avenue and Bond Street, which was then being used as a playground by local children. Asbury Park merchants resisted the building of the armory, claiming that if Bradley sold the property to the state the city would be losing taxes that would be collected if the location was used for a warehouse or similar commercial enterprise. In the end, the state won out and paid Bradley $18,750 for the property the armory building now stands on. In 1914, a construction contract was awarded by the State of New Jersey to the Berry-Goodwin Company of Philadelphia for $24,750. Construction was completed and the armory accepted by the state in 1915.

Although much of the state's National Guard was mobilized in response to a federal order on July 19, 1916, for duty in Arizona after Mexican revolutionary leader Pancho Villa crossed the border and attacked the town of Columbus, New Mexico, Company H and its regiment remained in New Jersey on alert for possible deployment.

Top: The Asbury Park Armory, built in 1916, in a postcard image from that era. The view is from Lake Avenue. *Courtesy of the Asbury Park Library.*

Bottom: Members of Company H of the 3rd Infantry Regiment, New Jersey National Guard, pose outside the Asbury Park Armory. Although the image is blurry, considering the style of the uniforms and the date of the armory's construction, this photograph was probably taken in 1915 or 1916. *Courtesy of VFW Post 1333.*

The rest of the Jersey Guardsmen returned from Arizona in autumn 1916, but in the summer of 1917, the entire National Guard was called to active duty for service in World War I. The men of Asbury Park's Company H traveled to Sea Girt, where they and the rest of the 3rd New Jersey's soldiers were sworn into federal service on July 25. The Jerseymen were shipped out to Camp McClellan in

Anniston, Alabama, where Company H added some Delaware Guardsmen and became Company E of the 114th U.S. Infantry regiment of the 29th Division. The company went on to fight with the 114th in the Meuse-Argonne Offensive in France in 1918 and returned to Asbury Park in 1919.

The people of Asbury Park, caught up in a nationwide patriotic propaganda campaign, were enthusiastic supporters of the American effort in World War I. Asbury Park women joined the Red Cross in large numbers, several male teachers from Asbury Park high school joined the military and two girls from the high school traveled to New York to join the Women's Land Army of America. The girls, enlisted as "farmerettes," ended up living in a communal rural barracks. "Clad in overalls, and wearing big straw hats," they worked on local farms in jobs ranging from weeding crops to cutting skunk cabbage in swamps "from eight in the morning to five in the evening for fifty cents a day."

The national patriotic rush occasioned by the conflict faded by 1920, giving way to a more cynical postwar era of prohibition, bootleg booze and crooked politics. The Asbury Park Armory eventually became home to Company G of the 114th Infantry Regiment, New Jersey National Guard, the successor unit to the old Companies A and H of the 3rd New Jersey Infantry, as well as to the staff of the 114th's Second Battalion. In September 1940, the New Jersey National Guard was called once again into federal service, ostensibly for a period of training. After December 7, 1941, that training turned into five years of war, and the men of Company G did not return to Asbury Park until 1945.

Although emptied by the departure of Company G, the armory soon became home to Company B of the New Jersey State Guard's 8th Battalion. The State Guard was a unit raised to replace the now-deployed National Guard in instances when the governor needed to call on the military. Company B was called to active duty within the

The armory's Lake Avenue entrance in 2012. It is now the home of VFW Post 1333. *Courtesy of Joseph Bilby.*

state in December 1941, when Governor Charles Edison mobilized his State Guard following the attack on Pearl Harbor. Deployed to temporarily guard the Route 9 Bridge over the Raritan River, Company B, along with the other units of the guard, was called up off and on for brief periods of service throughout the war, using the Asbury Park Armory as a home base.

In the post–World War II era, the Asbury Park Armory was returned to the New Jersey National Guard but was also used as a venue for occasional professional wrestling and boxing matches in the 1950s. In 2011, boxing returned to the building in the form of Police Athletic League matches.

In the 1960s, the National Guard abandoned the armory, turning it over to Harold Daley Post 1333, Veterans of Foreign Wars. As is customary, the post was named after a local soldier killed in action.

Harold Daley, who lived at 708 Main Street in Asbury Park, was a National Guardsman in Company H, 3rd New Jersey Infantry, before World War I and then served in Company E of the 114th Infantry. The twenty-one-year-old Daley was killed while fighting with Company E in the Bois d'Ormonde in France on October 12, 1918, a scant month before the war ended. Although other men born in Asbury Park were killed in action or died of disease in World War I, Daley was the only Asbury Park resident serving in the old Company H to lose his life in combat. The company lost other men, but they were not residents of Asbury Park.

The Daley Post, to this day the only Veterans of Foreign Wars post in existence that has a former armory building as its headquarters, sponsored the Asbury Park Hurricanes Drum and Bugle Corps, a junior corps based in Asbury Park. The Hurricanes wore black-and-gold cadet-style uniforms and competed in the Hudson Berkshire Drum and Bugle Corps Circuit. Most of the corps' instructors were veterans of the Hawthorne Caballeros Senior Drum and Bugle Corps.

Current Daley Post commander Lou Parisi is determined to maintain the post's integral and vital role in the local community. Post 1333 not only hosts its own meetings but also continues its long-standing public service role by providing space for community public events, including veterans' job fairs. The post has also served as a temporary home for Asbury Park's ReVision Theater Company and other organizations.

The old armory building's basement has been the home, since April 2011, of Brian Boyce's "Major B's General Quarters," an impressive professional-quality World War II diorama exhibit. From the hedgerows of Normandy to Iwo Jima's Mount Suribachi, Boyce's realistic and mesmerizing historical scenes capture the imagination of the visitor, bringing back a time long gone, when civilization hung in the balance and the American soldier was not found wanting.

An incident in the Normandy Campaign of 1944 re-created in diorama form by Brian Boyce at his "Major B's General Quarters" diorama and model museum in the armory basement. *Courtesy of Joseph Bilby.*

Boyce, a U.S. Navy veteran and longtime World War II hobbyist and master modeler, has displayed his dioramas and worked, over the years, with the Veterans Administration vocational rehabilitation therapy program, as well as the Brookdale Community College Center for World War II Studies and the National Guard Militia Museum of New Jersey Veterans' Oral History program, which has used the armory as an off-site interviewing venue. Combining oral history video testimony, photos and original research, Boyce has re-created crucial events of a number of veterans' service memories in three-dimensional form. In addition to its lifelike dioramas, "Major B's General Quarters" also houses a large number of individual models of World War II ships, planes, tanks and vehicles. It is open to the public.

Soldiers, veterans and members of the wider community have all made their marks on the Asbury Park Armory. The survivors

American Sherman tanks taking on the Normandy hedgerows as portrayed in another diorama at "Major B's General Quarters." *Courtesy of Joseph Bilby.*

of Asbury Park's Company A of the 3rd New Jersey Infantry, the first Asbury Park National Guardsmen, many of them Spanish-American War veterans, met at the building before attending one of their last reunions in Sea Girt, at the National Guard Training Center a few miles to the south, in 1948.

On November 11 of every year following World War I, the survivors of the 171 Company H men who marched off in 1917 assembled at the Asbury Park Armory to commemorate the end of that conflict and their 25 comrades who never returned. By 1978, only 16 veterans remained, and of them, only 9 were physically able to attend the reunion. The ceremony concluded, for a final time, with the recitation of a poem written by a deceased Company H soldier, former New Jersey governor Harold Hoffman of South Amboy, which read, in part:

> *Tonight we call the company roll*
> *Some lads do not respond*
> *They walk the starry outpost, out in the great beyond.*

Railroad Station

Main Street between Cookman and Bangs Avenues
GPS: 40° 13' 01 81" N, 74° 00' 50.19" W

It was a day of great civic pride in Asbury Park when the city unveiled its imposing new train station, a magnificent structure designed to usher in the city's status as a contemporary resort, much to the delight of modernizing mayor Clarence Hetrick. The station replaced what many had come to consider an outmoded Victorian-era oddity, referred to by many as a "dilapidated depot," after a period of "long agitation" by local influential citizens.

The year was 1922, a time of enormous political and social change and transformation across the country in the wake of World War I and Prohibition and its enabling Volstead Act, and the Central Railroad of New Jersey wanted to distance itself from the rustic wooden Queen Anne–style depot that had represented a tamer, less sophisticated era. And so the Asbury Park of the Founder, James A. Bradley, began to give way more rapidly, a year after his death, to Clarence Hetrick's innovative, more secular and up-to-date Jazz Age city.

The new and imposing structure, built at a cost of $200,000, was designed by architect Kenneth Tower, who rendered it in a Beaux-Arts design with Neoclassical detailing. The stately station towered over a large and sprawling parking plaza—automobiles were then fully complementing the transportation system they would eventually eclipse—that spanned the length of Main Street from Cookman to Bangs Avenues. The station was so impressive that Joshua Lionel Cowan used it as a prototype for building model Number 112 and subsequent Numbers 113 through 117, replica miniature stations used in layouts for his growing Lionel model train company located farther north in Hillside, New Jersey.

The original nineteenth-century Asbury Park railroad station, with freight and passenger depots. *Courtesy of the Asbury Park Library.*

The opulence of the building was not unusual for early twentieth-century train stations, when rail travel remained enormously popular, as well as practical, considering the lackluster national road network, despite growing competition from the automobile. New York's Penn Station and Grand Central Station—the latter designed by Whitney Warren, the New York architect subsequently responsible for Asbury Park's Berkeley-Carteret Hotel, Convention Hall and Casino—were contemporaries of the Asbury Park station.

Railroads came early to New Jersey, and the first functioning rail route in the state, a horse-drawn stretch of the Camden and Amboy between Bordentown and Hightstown, opened in 1831. Steam power came to the Camden and Amboy, which later became a notorious monopoly, in September 1833 with the locomotive John Bull. In the massive economic expansion following the Civil War, numerous railroads were built across the state, creating an extensive network of freight and passenger transportation.

The small New York and Long Branch Railroad played a pivotal role in opening up the wilderness of the Monmouth County, New Jersey Shore to vacationers in the post–Civil War era and allowed entrepreneurs like James A. Bradley to turn desolate stretches of scrub brush and sand into thriving resorts like Asbury Park. When Bradley first conceived the idea for an actual resort just north of the new summer camp meeting religious retreat of Ocean Grove, there was no direct railroad connection between the shore and the population centers to the north.

Travelers from northern New Jersey and New York, including Bradley himself, had to take a series of ferries, trains and stagecoaches to make the trip to the coast. Bradley was prescient, however, as the New York and Long Branch moved down the coast with the tourist trade, reaching Asbury Park in 1875. By 1885, the company's tracks, then jointly leased by the Pennsylvania Railroad and the Central Railroad of New Jersey, carried thirty

An engine pulls into the Victorian-era Asbury Park station. *Courtesy of the Asbury Park Library.*

trains a day from New York City and Newark "down the shore" during tourist season. A travel guide of the era described the journey down the coast aboard the trains as a "first class" one, noting that one could travel south aboard "a number of fast express trains with parlor cars."

If anything, summer train travel to the coast increased in the early twentieth century. In 1911, the Pennsylvania scheduled two extra trains a day on its New York and Long Branch run to accommodate an ever-growing number of tourists. It was a high time for passenger rail transport, and a train trip to the shore remained a preferable way to visit Asbury Park through the 1930s and even into the early post–World War II era. In those days, Asbury Park boasted two stations: a main one where the grand new station was built in 1922 and a North Asbury station in the northern part of town. There were periodic squabbles between the railroads and adjacent Ocean Grove, a strict Methodist enclave, regarding Sunday rail traffic at the main station, which was also the station for Ocean Grove and which the clergy found offensive. In the end, business won out over theology.

All things come to an end, and the age of mass train transportation to resort areas faded in the 1950s with significant improvements in the national road system, including the building of the Garden State Parkway in New Jersey, and the new mobility of a prosperous automobile-owning middle class. By the 1970s, the magnificent old Asbury Park station was no longer bustling with tourists and, like its humbler predecessor, was taking on an air of dilapidation. The station was demolished in 1978, to be eventually replaced with the present, far more modest structure. The new station, dedicated in June 1985, was named the James J. Howard Transportation Center after the congressman who secured the federal funds to make it possible, with the city's police station and municipal building taking up much of the ground where the old station and its parking area

The new large station erected in 1922, with expansive parking area, was used as a model for Lionel model train stations. *Courtesy of the Asbury Park Library.*

The subdued Transportation Center that replaced the grand 1922 station as it appears in 2012. *Courtesy of Joseph Bilby.*

once sprawled. Some vacationers continued to take the train to the shore, however, and in 1988, you could arrive in Asbury Park by rail and ride a shuttle bus from the station to the beach or to the Berkeley Hotel for two dollars.

In 1997, the Asbury Park City Council approved a plan to turn the station area into Station Square, a complex that, in addition to the train station, was to include a new bus transfer center, stores and offices. The New Jersey Economic Development Authority and the State Department of Transportation loaned the city $7.8 million to complete the transition. Today, although the bus transfer center gets considerable traffic and there is a long, low building labeled "Railroad Plaza" housing some small shops on the Memorial Drive side of the tracks, the grand design of 1997 appears largely unrealized.

The trains still stop at Asbury Park's main station; although the North Asbury station is still standing, it is no longer in use. The grand old days when droves of summer tourists swarmed into town from the station's trains are over, but the city's rail link to the outside world—now the property of the state-run New Jersey Transit—endures, and with the seemingly inevitable advent of high-speed trains in the future, it may well renew its former glory.

The Orchid Lounge (Demolished)

Springwood Avenue and Memorial Drive
GPS: 40° 12' 53.47" N, 74° 00' 56.37" W

At the outset of the twentieth century, Asbury Park's beach scene had its own type of music: the "wholesome" John Philip Sousa military-type band tunes provided by popular conductors such as

Arthur Pryor. On the city's West Side, however, an alluring new type of dance music thrived. Known as ragtime, its syncopated beat originated within the African American community and soon became an international sensation, as well as something of a threat to the more "proper" members of society—not the first time nor the last for such a music phenomenon in American history.

From the turn of the century onward, the West Side—home in the early 1900s to African Americans who provided the vital service engine of the city's tourist industry, Italian immigrants who came to town to build the seacoast trolley system and other marginalized residents of Asbury Park—proved a fertile creative ground for the local entertainment scene and was usually one step ahead of the musical mainstream. By the 1920s, ragtime, made more acceptable to the American middle class through cover songs often plagiarized by white composers and singers, began to give way to a new musical threat: jazz. One of the West Side's main thoroughfares, Springwood Avenue, was, as usual, ahead of the curve and boasted an array of sophisticated nightclubs where fun-seeking patrons shimmied to the seductive new rhythms while downing legally prohibited alcohol. The street was by then a gathering place for the city's thriving African-American community, and its music scene was rapidly becoming legendary as Jazz morphed into Rock and Roll in the post-World War II world. That creative groundswell reached its peak in the 1950s and '60s, when clubs like the Orchid Lounge, owned by former Asbury Park police officer Odyssey Moore, drew dazzling talent such as George Benson, Al Green and Rhonda Scott.

Like the other nightspots that lined Springwood Avenue, the Orchid Lounge drew an African American crowd who dressed up for the occasion. Davey Sancious, who grew up on the West Side, recalls men in dark suits with knotted ties and bejeweled women sporting chic hats. In her book *Asbury Park: A West Side Story*, Madonna Carter Jackson recalled, "Black people in Asbury Park worked

The site of the famed Orchid Lounge club, now an empty lot on the corner of Springwood Avenue and Memorial Drive. *Courtesy of Joseph Bilby.*

hard, played hard and always looked good." She remembered women dressed in beautiful dresses of satin and silk, complemented by "stiletto heels with French silk stockings." For the hardworking residents of the West Side, many of whom labored at backbreaking jobs in the hospitality industry, "singing, dancing, entertaining or being entertained was a pleasure after a long week of working at the shore restaurants and hotels," Jackson noted.

The creative talent headlining at the Orchid Lounge inspired not only its black audience but also young white performers who were eager to be inspired by the best cutting-edge entertainment. At a 2011 panel discussion on Asbury's musical heritage, renowned rock performer Southside Johnny Lyon recalled standing outside the club as a young man to listen raptly as B.B. King entertained inside.

As a showcase for show business luminaries, the Orchid Lounge was part of a larger Springwood Avenue universe that included hot nightspots like Cuba's Night Club, the Turf Club and the Madonna

Club. Headliners at these bustling nightspots included Ike and Tina Turner, Little Richard and Count Basie and his orchestra.

Springwood Avenue and the West Side were also creative training grounds for local talent. During the 1940s, gospel quartet singers were extremely popular, and two of the biggest West Side groups were the Golden Harmonaires and the Missionary Jubilaires. Arthur Morris, lead singer of the Golden Harmonaires, hosted a popular weekly gospel show on WJLK, the *Asbury Park Press* radio station, during which his group sang live.

Rhythm and blues singing groups hit their stride in the 1950s, and the roster of local African American talent included the Delcos, the Juveniles and the Mar-Keys. Bobby Thomas and the Vibranaires (later shortened to the Vibes) even scored a four-song recording session with Lexy "Flap" Handford's After Hours label in New York City. Although the group received little national airplay, they became local sensations thanks to their record deal. "We were like the Frankie Lymon and the Teenagers of our time," Thomas recalled, referring to an enormously popular 1950s singing group that performed at the city's Convention Hall during the decade.

Yet for all the creativity, showmanship and talent that thrived along Springwood Avenue and the West Side, the efforts went largely unheralded. Behind the glamour and sparkle was the bitter truth of de facto segregation, a fact of life in Asbury Park dating back to the days of the Founder, James A. Bradley, and only slightly modified during the era of Mayor Clarence Hetrick. In the mid-twentieth century, Asbury Park's black residents were still confined to a small section of beachfront and forced to enter schools though separate entrances than those used by white students. Aside from the occasional WJLK slot, the achievements and triumphs of West Side residents were largely ignored by the white mainstream media.

Such blatant injustice was repugnant to the black community, and by the 1960s, African Americans were increasingly frustrated with their lack of social and economic progress, locally as well as nationally. These feelings were apparent in numerous cities across the country, including Asbury Park, where black residents were still confined to the West Side and stymied by the lack of any real progress in the city. Matters came to a head on the evening of July 4, 1970, when a large gathering of black teens scuffled with police. Order was restored the next day, but by dusk, crowds had begun to assemble. Shortly after midnight, a group of about seventy-five teenagers broke into the Neptune Diner on Springwood Avenue. Police barricaded Springwood from Main Street—the dividing line between black and white Asbury—and the crowds forming along Springwood erupted into a wave of destruction.

As the rioting continued into the morning of July 6, city officials declared a state of emergency, calling on police from throughout the area for help. Within hours, the situation was under control, but by noon, fights had erupted again, and a fire broke out that destroyed the landmark Fisch's department store. Trouble continued into the next day, when an angry crowd of about two hundred people clashed with police.

Although rioting had subsided by Saturday, July 11, the devastated Springwood Avenue was an open wound that served as a disturbing visual reminder of the divide between most of Asbury Park's black and white populations. Overall, 180 persons had been injured and 167 arrested, and property damage had reached $4 million.

Ms. Carter recalled that her mother took 8mm movies of the riots but that her father, the well-respected West Side studio photographer Joseph A. Carter, wanted the footage destroyed. "The trashing of Springwood Avenue hurt him deeper than the fire that destroyed his studio in 1978," she wrote in her book. If you drive west on Springwood Avenue today, you will see vacant lots and a few modern structures constructed since the rioting. Here and there, though, you can catch a view of the old

Springwood, a short row of early twentieth-century buildings, as though you have stepped back in time.

Although the Orchid Lounge, on the border between what was black and white Asbury Park, was not destroyed in the riots, its surroundings were devastated, signaling that the legendary club's days were numbered. The vibrant artistic lifeblood of Springwood Avenue had been drained away, and the Orchid Lounge soon faded with it. Today, an empty lot stands where entertainers once enthralled appreciative crowds.

Yet better times may be ahead. After years of neglect, Asbury Park officials have formulated a detailed redevelopment plan for Springwood Avenue that would restore the thoroughfare to its former glory. In a nod to its illustrious past as an entertainment venue, city planners will allow nightclubs to operate in the redevelopment zone. Clubs like the Orchid Lounge may once again enthrall audiences with the type of talent that made Springwood Avenue legendary.

Tour 3

SOUTH ASBURY

THE CASINO (PARTIALLY DEMOLISHED)

South end of the boardwalk
www.youtube.com/watch?v=xKzm9BlVPv4
GPS: 40° 13' 04.34" N, 74° 00' 02.63" W

In early 1903, Asbury Park's merchants and politicians successfully pressured James A. Bradley to sell his boardwalk, with its bathhouses, pavilions, fishing pier and band shell, to the city for $100,000. By the summer of that year, the southernmost of Bradley's deteriorating one-story pavilions was gone, replaced by a two-story Casino designed by Asbury Park architect William Cottrell. Cottrell's Casino, which cost the city fathers $60,000 to construct, was not, as the name might imply, a gambling establishment but a large public hall that also held a bathhouse and boardwalk amusements and concessions, eventually including a candy store featuring saltwater taffy.

A view north along the boardwalk through the original Casino in the early twentieth century. *Courtesy of the Asbury Park Library.*

In 1928, just a month prior to Mayor Clarence Hetrick's public criticism of Asbury Park's lack of new construction in comparison with that of rival Atlantic City to the south, the Casino was incinerated in a fire of "undetermined origin." As with the Fifth Avenue Pavilion to the north, the firm of Warren and Wetmore of New York City was contracted to replace it with a more modern building. Whitney Warren, the same Beaux-Arts architect who was responsible for the Berkeley-Carteret Hotel and Convention Hall, designed a new structure that was built in 1929–30. Although there may have been some shady dealing with the awarding of a no-bid contract, Clarence Hetrick knew he wanted quality, and in Warren, he got the absolute best.

The new Casino, constructed of concrete and steel, was indeed a far superior structure to its wooden-frame predecessor and a perfect mate for Convention Hall to the north. The building's solid extension over the beach served as a venue for trade shows, concerts and convention-oriented affairs. A boardwalk arcade was spanned by an arched roof that connected to another semicircular section that housed amusements and refreshment stands and also boasted an attached circular merry-go-round building with a stylish copper roof. The wooden carousel horses were provided by the Philadelphia Toboggan Company and were delivered in 1932.

Hetrick's plan to make Asbury Park a year-round tourist destination to compete with Atlantic City for the convention trade required that his new boardwalk buildings offer winter warmth, and Warren complied with a unique heating plant design. The plant, which adjoined the Casino complex on its eastern side, was a decidedly exotic-looking building, with a tower based on a similar structure that Warren had developed for the Catholic University of Louvain in Belgium when it was rebuilt following its destruction in World War I. It would heat the boardwalk pavilions and Convention Hall as well.

The replacement Casino constructed in 1929 by Mayor Hetrick as it appeared in the 1930s, looking east. The circular part of the building houses a merry-go-round. The chimney of the heating plant is visible to the right. *Courtesy of the Asbury Park Library.*

The Casino building project also served a less than noble motive on Hetrick's part. On the whole, the mayor was a progressive politician for early twentieth-century America who had actually gained the support of Asbury Park's African American community by saving an innocent black man from lynching while he was serving as county sheriff. Although Hetrick did not seriously challenge the overall pervasive racism of the era, he did, however, seem a significant improvement over James A. Bradley in racial matters. The Founder had restricted Asbury Park's African Americans, without whose labor his resort would have collapsed, from using his privately owned beach and boardwalk to a few evening hours; Hetrick provided the black community with their own time unrestricted but segregated beach on the south side of the Casino, conveniently blocked from the view of white bathers to the north by the building and the heating plant. In a more positive

The new Casino as seen from the northwest. As with Convention Hall, a good part of the building extended over the beach. *Courtesy of the Asbury Park Library.*

action, Hetrick made sure a significant number of service jobs at the Casino were open to Asbury Park's African Americans and even allowed African American–owned concessions on the south side of the Casino.

Hetrick's massive projects quite literally broke the bank for Asbury Park. Taking on bond debt of over $4 million on the eve of the Depression subsequently staggered the city. Throughout the 1930s, the boardwalk did not generate enough revenue to advertise itself, and even the Baby Parade for which Asbury Park had become famous in the early twentieth century was cancelled in 1932. The still-rich went elsewhere for vacations, and the vacationing middle class went broke. The only bright spot in Asbury Park's financial picture during the Depression was provided by the macabre appearance of the burned-out *Morro Castle* on the beach by Convention Hall. During the months that the blackened ghost ship remained near the beach, an estimated 250,000 visitors came to Asbury Park to see it, and merchants took advantage of the public's morbid curiosity concerning the wreck over the winter of 1934–35 to offer food and entertainment to the crowds.

Although World War II brought the country out of the Depression, it did not herald a revival for Asbury Park and other New Jersey Shore resorts, as food rationing hampered the restaurant business and gas rationing put a heavy crimp in the tourist travel industry. One bright spot during the wartime years was the New York Yankee baseball team's spring training session, which was held in Asbury Park in 1943 due to wartime transportation restrictions on the team. Many Asbury Park hotels were taken over for military use, housing soldiers, transient British sailors and officer candidates; the latter provided convenient manpower to assist local authorities during the destructive hurricane that struck the Jersey Shore in 1944. In addition to hosting very limited tourist traffic during the war, the boardwalk

The Casino merry-go-round, circa 1960. *Courtesy of the Asbury Park Library.*

In 2012, the merry-go-round annex sits empty. *Courtesy of Joseph Bilby.*

had to shut down at night as dim-out and blackout conditions were imposed to hinder German submarines lurking offshore, especially in 1942. The oft-told story that the boardwalk vendors of Asbury Park and other shore towns defied those orders and that their actions were responsible for the heavy toll on Allied shipping off the coast early in the war is totally apocryphal and readily disproved by a reading of the minutes of New Jersey governor Charles Edison's War Cabinet, which are available online courtesy of the New Jersey State Archives.

Postwar prosperity brought Asbury Park back, both as a vacation venue and as a local business and shopping hub. The Casino and its carousel and amusements—the first Asbury Park attraction a visitor encountered on walking into the city along the boardwalk from Ocean Grove—delighted many a 1950s child. Even families who summered in other Monmouth County shore towns came to Asbury Park for the amusements, boardwalk food and evening excitement. Asbury Park was back! It seemed the ride would never end. But it did.

The Casino suffered as much as, if not more than, other attractions in the city's downward spiral of the 1980s. Amusement venues were abandoned. The copper roofing was stripped off the building for sale as scrap, and the exposed roof wood began to rot. In 1990, the Casino's renowned carousel was sold to Family Kingdom Amusement Park in Myrtle Beach, South Carolina, where it continues to operate. Its former home housed a downscale flea market for a decade.

In 2007, the eastern side of the Casino building, the section that reached out into the surf on pilings, was demolished. Attempts have been made to save what is left. A new metal roof, mimicking the old green-toned aged copper, has been installed on the former home of the carousel, and there are rumored plans to save the remainder of the structure. Unlike Convention Hall to the north, however,

The ghostly Casino as it appears today, looking north along the boardwalk. The portion extending over the beach has been demolished, and the remainder hopefully awaits restoration. *Courtesy of Joseph Bilby.*

the Beaux-Arts Casino, with Whitney Warren's medieval towers still standing and marking the long-abandoned boardwalk heating plant that adjoins it, presents a sad and haunting sight, leading one observer to comment that the scene evoked a cameo image of a bombed-out World War II European city and another to comment that it embodied the theme of, appropriately enough, the Bruce Springsteen song "My City of Ruins."

But better days have come for much of Asbury Park, and there is hope for the Casino as well. It is an iconic building in an iconic town, and what remains of it deserves to be saved.

MAYFAIR THEATER (DEMOLISHED)

Lake Avenue and St. James Place (301 Lake Avenue)
www.asburyboardwalk.com/pic/mayfair/m1.htm
GPS: 40° 13' 02.45" N, 74° 00' 13.82" W

In the eyes of entertainment impresario Walter Reade, it was to be a movie theater like no other in New Jersey, a majestic tribute to the glittering world of cinema. And when the opulent Mayfair, a million-dollar Spanish-Moorish palace on Lake Avenue, opened its doors in 1927, his vision appeared to be justified.

An elegantly dressed crowd of some 1,500 guests attended the theater's grand opening on a warm August evening, thrilled by the ornate architecture and luxurious ambience. After passing through giant grill doors at the entrance, visitors entered the spacious lobby. The room was dominated by a large Spanish-style well, surrounded by floral pieces, huge vases and Spanish works of art. Inside the auditorium, guests were impressed by the seats of Moroccan leather with hand-woven tapestry backs. There were 1,260 seats in the theater, and a reporter noted, "There is hardly a seat in the house from which the spectator cannot see the screen as good as those seated in the very center of the house near the front." To provide the "mood music" so integral to the silent film experience of the time, the Mayfair boasted a Moller organ featuring six thousand possible controls, with a separate keyboard connected to tower chimes.

Sitting in the theater, patrons were awestruck by the hidden lights that created a scene of clouds and stars on the expansive ceiling. Five drop curtains were positioned between the screen and footlights; one of the curtains was red and studded with rhinestones, and the others were of varying colors. During an era when most people suffered in the heat with the aid of an electric fan at most, the Mayfair's patrons enjoyed a modern ventilation and cooling system.

The Mayfair Theater, perhaps the classiest movie theater in New Jersey in its heyday. It was demolished when it became too expensive to maintain. Condos have since been built on the site. *Courtesy of Don Stine.*

Basking in the compliments of the crowd on that momentous grand opening night, Reade vowed to provide only the best in entertainment. "Their words of praise encourage me and I am more than ever determined to give the people of this section the best possible in the Mayfair," he pledged.

Certainly, Reade had the experience and show-business savvy to make good on his promise. Born Walter Rosenberg, the former necktie salesman began his show-business career as manager of several vaudeville theaters in New York. By the early 1900s, the aspiring entrepreneur had cast his ambitious eyes on the thriving resort of Asbury Park, where he acquired the Rialto, a vaudeville house on Main Street just south of Springwood Avenue. The storefront theater was frequented by members of the West Side's working-class Italian American community and, in this era of transitional entertainment, featured silent movies as well as live performances.

In 1910, the increasingly successful Reade entered into a partnership with Asbury Park real estate entrepreneur Hugh Kinmonth for a new downtown theater. They opened the Savoy, a combination office and movie house building, on Mattison Avenue in March 1912. Yet Rosenberg's ambitions were much grander than simply owning a few theaters. Just as the film industry was mushrooming into a multimillion-dollar business, so were Rosenberg's plans to become a heavy hitter in the entertainment world. In 1917, he broke ground on a new theater at the corner of Cookman Avenue and St. James Place. The new movie house, regally dubbed the St. James, featured 2,300 seats in brown plush and a theater organ to provide mood music for the adventure and romance onscreen. The opening of the St. James also marked a time of personal reinvention for Rosenberg, who officially changed his name to the more elegant Walter Reade; the name Reade topped the St. James marquee, and both Reade and his equally entrepreneurial son Walter Jr. would be identified by their new names from then on.

As the country entered the bubbly decade of the 1920s, movies became a national cult, and the ever-more-opulent theaters were their shrines. Once-anonymous film actors became stars in their own right, from the beatific Mary Pickford to the romantic John Barrymore. Moviegoers were able to lose themselves in the dark, thrilling to the exploits of flapper Joan Crawford, Latin lover Rudolph Valentino and beloved comic Charlie Chaplin. Hollywood became a fabled land of wealth and glamour, and an entire industry of related businesses, from movie fan magazines to film-inspired fashion, was launched.

Inspired by this dynamic era of dazzling success, the confident Reade decided to build his most magnificent movie house ever— the Mayfair. Designed by architect Thomas Lamb, the cream-colored theater was distinguished by its elaborate exterior of hand-sculpted Spanish stucco, with outside balconies outlined by arches. The majestic structure dominated Lake Avenue, and at night, the illuminated theater building looked like a fantasy palace casting its lights onto the placid waters of Wesley Lake and staid Ocean Grove beyond.

The theater's fantastic architecture and luxurious amenities made it a must-see destination for movie lovers, and for decades, the Mayfair was a symbol of Hollywood's power and allure. Just as the film industry prospered, so did the Reades. After Walter Sr.'s death in 1952, young Walter took firm control of the family's finances. By 1963, Walter Jr. had amassed six theaters in Asbury Park alone, just a small part of an empire that totaled eighty-nine theaters in New Jersey, neighboring states and beyond.

Times, however, were changing, and the glamorous movie palaces of yesterday were beginning to look like dusty, over-exaggerated relics from an out-of-touch past. The increasingly popular drive-in theater was the antithesis of the movie palace, and its rowdy informality made the old film houses resemble someone's endearing but hopelessly dated spinster aunt. Reade himself was aware of changing tastes and entered into negotiations to build his first suburban theater in neighboring Ocean Township. In 1970, he closed the Mayfair and St. James to save on the enormous heating bills generated by the cavernous structures.

The younger Reade died in 1973, leaving behind a substantial pile of debt, in part due to the shifting nature of the movie theater business. A year later, the Walter Reade Organization announced plans to demolish the Mayfair and St. James. "The harsh reality of today's economy in this energy crisis world precludes the possibility of efficiently remodeling or modernizing them," said Sheldon Gunsberg, president of the organization. Despite the efforts of the Save the Mayfair Committee, which offered $100,000 for the structure, the demolition moved forward. "Mayfair to Die Thursday" the *Asbury Park Press* declared on December 3, 1974.

The destruction of the Mayfair truly marked the end of an era, for the palatial theater represented a time gone by of movie glamour and artifice, qualities that seemed quaint and pretentious in an era of gritty filmmaking and down-to-earth actors. The Mayfair's mystique lives on, however, in the minds of film aficionados who cherish the golden era of moviemaking.

In fact, one Indianapolis man has gone a step further, building a 1920s-style theater in his home and furnishing it with numerous items salvaged from the Mayfair. Eric von Grimmenstein III remodeled a series of rooms to re-create a movie house from Hollywood's golden age. The layout includes a box office, concession area, lobby and theater, where most of the Mayfair artifacts, including a chandelier, are displayed. Grimmenstein found the Mayfair items, including seven-foot-high metal doors, sconces and light fixtures, at a Philadelphia antique dealer's establishment and lovingly restored the rusted, neglected treasures. So the spirit of the Mayfair lives on, in a faraway place, the subject of suitably appropriate romantic nostalgia.

PALACE AMUSEMENTS (DEMOLISHED)

Kingsley Street and Lake Avenue
www.palaceamusements.com/save_tillie.html
www.youtube.com/watch?v=buLTxQuam_c
GPS: 40° 13' 03.48" N, 74° 00' 08.87" W

Almost anyone of a certain age who grew up at or vacationed on the New Jersey Shore has a vivid memory of the Palace, that beloved, garish shrine to seaside amusements that mesmerized its visitors, in one form or another, for more than one hundred years. By the 1950s, the ever-changing Palace had expanded to a sprawling expanse of funhouses, a shooting gallery, games of chance, a carousel and a majestic Ferris wheel that dominated the Asbury Park skyline. At night, its gaudy neon lights and the grinning countenance of Tillie, the impish clown who winked impudently at passersby, quickened the pulses of every young person who came in search of excitement and thrills.

Well into the 1960s and early 1970s, the Palace remained a magical destination for the young and young at heart. Asbury Park merchant James Kaufman remembers carefree times with friends at age ten, when his parents would drop him off at the Palace while they enjoyed more subdued boardwalk pleasures. Clutching their strings of tickets, Kaufman and his buddies would race through the cavernous amusement hall, heading first to the Skee-Ball arcade and working their way through the bumper cars, funhouses and the Ferris wheel. He can still recall the tantalizing scents of cotton candy and peanuts mixed with the pungent smell of the oil and diesel fuel used to lubricate and power the rides.

When Kaufman returned with his nephew to the Palace in 1988, he beheld a different, sobering scenario. Although it was a beautiful spring day, the Palace was deserted, its darkened interior lifeless and depressing. Asbury Park's declining status as a pleasure destination had sapped the Palace of its clientele, and twenty years after Kaufman's melancholy visit, the building was destroyed, despite the organized protests of impassioned preservationists. Today, a parking lot marks the spot where glittering lights once lured visitors into a lighthearted world of tawdry thrills.

The Palace saga begins with the vision of amusements impresario Ernest Schnitzler, a German-born entrepreneur who capitalized on Asbury Park's emergence as a premier summer resort by constructing a four-sided Victorian building at the corner of Lake Avenue

Palace Amusements, once a tourist highlight with its wide variety of attractions and games, including bumper cars, after its closing. A battered Tillie still adorned the building. It was demolished soon afterward. *Courtesy of Harry Ziegler.*

and Kingsley Street. The elegant structure, with its wood frame doors fitted with colored glass, was designed to provide "refined amusement" for city founder James A. Bradley's comfortably middle-class family crowd that disembarked in droves from Asbury Park's railroad station each summer. A flag that fluttered from the roof heralded the enterprise's main draw, an elaborate merry-go-round crafted by Charles I.D. Looff, one of the country's eminent carousel builders. The three-row machine was adorned with hand-carved stationary animals, and despite several fires, the attraction remained in various forms until the Palace was destroyed. The carousel animals escaped destruction but, like their counterparts across the way at the Casino, were sold off, never to return.

Another one of the amusement complex's signature attractions, the Ferris wheel, was introduced by Schnitzler after a competitor announced plans to construct a fifty-foot "Observation Roundabout"

Where the Palace once was is now a parking area with condos beyond in 2012. *Courtesy of Joseph Bilby.*

next door to the Palace. After that conspicuous red, yellow and white wooden wheel opened in 1892, Schnitzler retaliated by building a bigger wheel with more passenger carriages and an observation platform that provided magnificent views of Asbury Park and Ocean Grove. The mammoth, seventy-four-foot-high iron structure opened in 1895, and soon after, the owners of the competing wheel dismantled it in defeat. For decades, Schnitzler's Ferris wheel dominated the city skyline and was little changed at the time it was dismantled prior to the Palace's demolition.

By the early twentieth century, the Palace was considered one of the most breathtaking amusement centers in the region. Schnitzler added to the complex's luster by constructing an elaborate maze of mirrors just north of the carousel. On warm summer nights, delighted revelers thronged the brilliantly illuminated building, wandering through the deceptive mirror maze and thrilling to the dazzling view atop the Ferris wheel observation platform, watching the milling crowds below. As one editor raved, the Palace was truly "the largest, most unique and most complete" amusement park on the Atlantic coast. Schnitzler continued to operate the business until the mid-1920s, when he sold it to August M. Williams.

Williams managed to steer the Palace through the grim Depression years, adding some innovative attractions such as a walk-through fun house with a rotating barrel and "surprise" drafts of air that startled patrons. In another effort to provide some memorable thrills, Williams introduced a "dark ride" known as Ghost Town—perhaps singularly appropriate to the dismal 1930s—which carried passengers in cars along electrified tracks through a labyrinth of dark tunnels and frightening encounters.

Such expansion efforts, however, were minor compared to the innovations of the Palace's next owners, Edward H. Lange and Zimel Resnick. Lange, who fell in love with Asbury Park during a visit in 1926, worked at a number of oceanfront establishments before teaming with Resnick to purchase the Palace in 1938. The ambitious duo were firm believers in aggressively updating and expanding the business, and the two entrepreneurs were quick to expand the building, purchasing property north of the Ferris wheel and building an addition to house new arcade games that had captured the public's fancy, such as Skee-Ball and pinball. During the 1940s, they also replaced Ghost Town with a more elaborate dark ride, the Haunted Caverns, which sent screaming passengers hurtling through the darkness as they encountered a series of spine-tingling scenes, from the devil pushing a man into a fire to the chilling sight of a hanging man.

The most impressive and enduring changes, however, were yet to come. Undaunted by the potential shifting tastes of pleasure-seekers in the mid-1950s, when superhighways like the Garden State Parkway made newer, shinier resorts farther south more easily available to tourists, Lange and Resnick embarked on their most ambitious undertaking to date. In 1956, they expanded the Palace by more than seventeen thousand square feet, creating open spaces supported by concrete block walls and adorned with murals that, to this day, are considered iconic symbols of Asbury Park. The various images, illuminated in bawdy neon, included the grinning visage of Tillie, a clown named in honor of Coney Island amusements impresario George Cornelius Tilyou. Two fifteen-foot-high renderings of the loony face graced the eastern and western ends of the building, winking invitingly. Other distinctive images included two huge Auto Skooters carrying their passengers into a head-on collision.

In the decades that followed, although Asbury's fortunes began a slow decline, the Palace remained a top draw. Even into the 1960s and 1970s, many of the rides remained a seemingly endless source of thrills and entertainment for teens of the era. The Whacky Shack, Orient Express, Olympic Bobs and Auto Skooters, popularly known as "bumper cars" to most folks, were just a few of the amusements that delighted thousands. Despite the Palace's allure, however, operating the establishment in the midst of an increasingly bleak and sometimes dangerous urban landscape finally took its toll on Lange and Resnick, and they sold the property to brothers Sam and Henry Vaccaro in 1986.

The Vaccaros had great plans for the Palace, as for other sites in Asbury Park, and invested heavily in the operation. They added new rides and, perhaps most significantly, opened a rock-and-roll museum that housed an enormous collection of memorabilia from Asbury Park's rich musical scene. The museum became a must-see destination that warranted intensive media coverage and attracted a diverse group of musical greats ranging from Bruce Springsteen to Bo Diddley.

Despite those bright beginnings, however, a series of economic and legal mishaps forced the Vaccaros to close the Palace in 1989 and hand ownership over to developer Joseph Carabetta, who failed to maintain the property. The legendary Palace was closed and eviscerated, its rides sold to various buyers. By 2001, the abandoned building was a crumbling monument to another era. Despite the impassioned efforts of the Save Tillie organization, a group of devoted advocates dedicated to preserving the Palace, the landmark, despite being on both state and federal registers of historic places, was demolished in 2008.

Yet the Palace lives on in spirit today, its memory kept alive through the efforts of Save Tillie, whose members now maintain a meticulously and vividly detailed website that chronicles the Palace's illustrious history, complete with rare photos and illustrations.

It also endures through the bits and pieces preserved by those who remain fascinated by the legendary amusement hall. James Kaufman now displays his collection of precious Palace remnants at his business, Flying Saucers, a retro collectibles store on Cookman Avenue. Mixed in with vintage magazines and '50s kitchen sets are a variety of Palace memorabilia that include the "L" from the "Palace Amusements" letters that lit up the exterior, a piece of the original wall, brass rings from the carousel and a painted wooden Palace Amusements sign that hung inside the building. In the same mall that houses Kaufman's store, only steps away on the lower level, is a restored photo booth from the Palace's heyday. And throughout the city, the grinning image of Tillie adorns sweatshirts, coffee mugs, refrigerator magnets and a host of other merchandise. You can even catch an outdoor glimpse of Tillie himself at the Wonder Bar, down Ocean Avenue across the street from McLoone's, the former boardwalk Howard Johnson's, where a reproduction painting adorns the club's exterior.

The dazzling lights and thrilling rides may be gone, but the spirit of Palace Amusements, an architectural icon that epitomized the carefree allure of Asbury Park, lives on.

CHARMS BUILDING (DEMOLISHED)

401 Monroe Avenue
www.youtube.com/watch?v=JQcnum0MvoA
GPS: 40° 13' 04.40" N, 74° 00' 23.05" W

Like the Phoenix, the majestic four-story building on Monroe Avenue seemed destined to repeatedly rise from the ashes, saving itself from oblivion through constant reinvention. Originally built as a lavish home for the Benevolent and Protective Order of Elks Lodge 128, the building assumed unlikely new identities as both a candy factory and iconic gay disco venue during its almost one-hundred-year history. It seemed that no matter what function it served, the Charms building, as it was commonly known, was destined to remain an elegant part of Asbury's downtown for years to come.

Despite the pleas of ardent preservationists, however, in December 2009, like many other treasured city landmarks in Asbury Park, it fell to the wrecker's ball. After thirteen years of vacancy, time had ravaged the once-exquisite landmark. Cracked stucco, broken windows and a huge chunk of missing cornice were among the evident signs of decay, and city officials deemed the building in danger of collapse.

The building's demolition (see link above) drew the ire of both the Asbury Park Historical Society and Preservation New Jersey, the latter an influential lobbying group that had placed the Charms building on its 2009 list of historic sites. Recognizing the building as "a potentially ideal transitional link" between the downtown and oceanfront, the group described the structure as a "splendid example of the Classical Revival style with Beaux Arts detail." With its prominent arched and Palladian windows, cast-iron balustrades and balconettes, the building was "a quintessential example of

The Elks Lodge, seen here in the 1920s, was later the Charms Candy factory and then became the M&K, an iconic watering hole for gay tourists in the 1980s. *Courtesy of Don Stine.*

the best of Asbury Park's historic commercial architecture," the organization noted.

Certainly, the Charms building had played a significant role in the history of Asbury Park, beginning with its construction in 1914 as an Elks lodge. The clubhouse soon doubled in size with nearly half a million dollars in construction and furnishings, including a social hall on the second floor that served as a small convention venue. During its twenty-six-year run, the Elks headquarters served an elite clientele of local movers and shakers, with a membership including Asbury Park bandleader Arthur Pryor and Charles Fitkin (for whom Fitkin Hospital, now Jersey Shore Medical Center, was named). As Elks, the men were committed to serving the community, and the organization helped area children with special needs, providing a clinic on the lodge's fourth floor staffed with doctors and nurses. In addition to their philanthropic efforts, the members also found time to enjoy the lodge's numerous amenities, which included four bowling alleys, a gymnasium and restaurants.

These men were part of a prestigious group that owed its origins to an English music hall performer who came to New York to seek his fortune in 1867. Thanks to his magnetic personality, Charles Algernon Sidney Vivian soon presided over a social group of entertainers who dubbed themselves the Jolly Corks. When a Jolly Cork died shortly before Christmas, leaving his family destitute, the other members decided they needed to create a more enduring organization to serve those in need. In 1868, they established the Benevolent and Protective Order of Elks and elected Vivian to head it.

Although political infighting resulted in Vivian's eventual ouster from the organization's leadership, his legacy of service lived on, and Elks chapters were established across the country. During World War I, the Elks funded and equipped the first two field hospitals in France and raised money for the Salvation Army's frontline canteens, among other efforts. Their loans to forty thousand returning servicemen for college, rehabilitation and vocational education were the precursor of the World War II–era GI Bill.

The building remained a hub of Elks activity until 1940, when the organization, strapped by the financial aftermath of the Depression, moved to a private house in north Asbury Park. The structure then entered its second incarnation as home to a candy empire. Walter W. Reid Jr., president of the Charms Candy Company of Bloomfield, New Jersey, opened a second packaging and administrative operation in the former Elks lodge partly because Asbury Park provided an easier commute than Bloomfield from his Allenhurst home. In addition to candies, the business also produced medicines for pharmaceutical companies. Once-glorious lodge rooms were now used as office space.

Perhaps the most colorful chapter in the building's history was to follow, when Paul Wisnewski transformed the once again abandoned

Elks-Charms building into a glittering disco that would become a staple of Asbury Park's burgeoning gay nightlife. Wisnewski had previously operated a gay complex know as the M&K across the street, and he christened his new nightclub with the same initials. The once-staid structure now became a multilevel nightclub with flashing lights as patrons danced to the strains of Donna Summer and numerous other disco artists echoing through its cavernous halls.

Wisnewski's investment came at a time when Asbury Park was enjoying a surging popularity with gay tourists from New York and Philadelphia. The M&K joined a community of other gay bars that catered to tourists and locals alike during the 1970s and 1980s. Several of them, now demolished, lined Cookman Avenue, including Archie's, a neighborhood bar, and the Odyssey, a disco that rivaled the M&K for its glitzy disco atmosphere. On warm

The site of the Elks Lodge, in 2012 a vacant lot. *Courtesy of Joseph Bilby.*

summer nights, patrons walked casually from club to club, while the insistent "thump" of dance music blared from bars, radios and eight-tracks.

As Asbury Park's decline accelerated in the late 1980s and early 1990s, however, its appeal to gay tourists also decreased, and the Charms building entered its last chapter as an abandoned relic of more prosperous times. Sadly, the Charms building's destruction in 2009 came at a time when Asbury Park was enjoying a renaissance and when members of the gay community, who had contributed to the M&K's success, were playing a key role in reenergizing the city. Numerous gay residents invested in restoring homes, while entrepreneurs renovated key commercial properties. Renowned record producer Shep Pettibone, an industry name of note who collaborated with artists such as Madonna and George Michael, rehabilitated the aging Empress Motel on Ocean Avenue and transformed it into a glittering nightclub/hotel complex that caters to gay tourists. Other venues such as Georgie's, a neighborhood bar that bills itself as a local Cheers, also provide entertainment options for the gay crowd.

In addition, traces of the gay community's past survive. The iconic Rainbow Room sign, which once graced the exterior of the Albion Hotel, has been restored by the Asbury Park Historical Society and is on display in the city's James J. Howard Transportation Center. The neon sign was a familiar sight for patrons of the Albion during its heyday as a gay venue. "The restored sign will serve as a reminder of the importance of the gay community in the history and rebirth of Asbury Park," said Carol Torre, former Albion owner.

Unfortunately, the Charms building never had the chance to become another one of the lovingly restored landmarks lining Asbury's downtown and beachfront. But its vibrant legacy—from civic-minded Elks lodge to bustling candy-making company to legendary disco—lives on.

The Civil War Soldier Monument

Intersection of Cookman and Grand Avenues
GPS: 40° 13' 23.92" N, 74° 00' 28.84" W

At the time of the Civil War, there was no Asbury Park. While New Jersey's soldiers fought and died for the Union far to the south in Virginia, the Carolinas and Georgia, the area the city by the sea would eventually occupy was but rolling sand dunes covered with wind-twisted shrubs and waving beach grasses kissed by Atlantic tides, largely inaccessible to vacationers and with little to recommend it for year-round residency. And yet the city features a Civil War monument, of the type usually erected in the postwar period to honor the soldiers a municipality sent off to war. How that monument, guarded by what are some rare antique artillery pieces, came to be, therefore, provides a story unique to Asbury Park.

James A. Bradley's Civil War statue, situated near the boardwalk at the end of Asbury Avenue. Automobiles in the picture suggest that this photograph dates from the early twentieth century. *Courtesy of Joseph Bilby.*

The city's founder, James A. Bradley, inspired by the thought of creating a family resort, bought the seemingly barren landscape in 1871. His wish came true, and in the years that followed, Asbury Park became a popular resort patronized by an increasingly affluent postwar American middle class. There were, unsurprisingly, a number of veterans of the then-recent conflict among the tourists. As the city expanded and businesses catering to the vacationers—as well as an increasing population in Asbury's hinterlands—prospered, so did the number of year-round veteran residents.

In the late nineteenth century, the notably eccentric Bradley scattered "interesting artifacts," including old stagecoaches, circus animal cages and other detritus, along the beach and boardwalk he personally owned to educate and entertain visitors, particularly children. A Civil War soldier statue not only fulfilled Bradley's

A pre-1898 parade in Asbury Park. The cavalry troop is a New Jersey National Guard unit, most likely from Red Bank. *Courtesy of the Asbury Park Library.*

educational criteria but could also serve as a sign that veterans, a desirable tourist demographic, were welcomed in his resort. Although the details of its acquisition are murky, there is no doubt that Bradley acquired such a statue and sited it in a small park near the boardwalk and a bathing pavilion at the east end of Asbury Avenue. The first firm reference to a soldier statue in that location is in an 1889 tour guide.

In the past, it was universally believed that Bradley's statue later became the current monument, but recent research makes this seem unlikely. Some stories date the Bradley figure to the 1870s, but this is unlikely as well, according to students of Civil War veteran statuary. The "soldier at rest" configuration was a generic late nineteenth-century product, turned out by the thousands for local memorials or even individual grave markers, in slightly varying forms and constructed of different materials, from zinc to bronze, depending on the amount of money purchasers wanted to spend. Although surviving images of the Bradley statue in its location near the beach indicate it is in the standard and common "at rest" pose, they date from the early twentieth century, and one postcard image includes automobiles. The ultimate fate of Bradley's statue, or what it was made of, is unknown. He did contribute twenty-five dollars to the current memorial's fund.

The official Asbury Park Civil War memorial statue, located in a pocket-sized park at the junction of Cookman and Grand Avenues, sits high atop a granite column donated by Civil War veteran George W. Potts of Ocean Grove and was formally dedicated on Memorial Day 1893. (For years afterward, the statue was often referred to as "old George Potts.") Potts had served as a lieutenant in the Twenty-first New York Artillery Battery and had the barrel of an artillery piece partially buried in his front yard as a war trophy. The dedication was accompanied by much fanfare, including a parade attended by the multitude of fraternal orders of the day, including the Tecumseh Tribe of Redmen, the Odd Fellows and the Order of Foresters, as well as veterans. The crowd listened to a dedicatory address by Commander H.L. Hartshorne of the New Jersey Department, Grand Army of the Republic, the national Civil War Union veterans' organization. The event was sponsored by the members of Asbury Park's Caldwell K. Hall Post of the Grand Army and Women's Relief Corps No. 25. The Women's Relief Corps was a ladies' auxiliary of the Grand Army.

The inscription on the plaque at the base of the granite column reads:

In Memory
Of Those Who Fought
In
Defense of the Union.

War of Rebellion
1861–1865

Erected by
C.K. Hall Post
No. 41 G.A.R. Dept. of N.J.
And Women's
Relief Corps No. 25

The Hall post was named after Lieutenant Colonel Caldwell K. Hall, a veteran of the 14th New Jersey Infantry, a Civil War regiment raised in central New Jersey in 1862. Hall, a Trenton attorney, was badly wounded at the battle of Monocacy, Maryland, in July 1864 and died in 1870. Although some have asserted that the statue was erected specifically to pay tribute to the soldiers of the 14th, many of whom were recruited in Monmouth County, no doubt tying that

The Civil War monument located in the mini-park at Grand and Cookman Avenues. This was the monument dedicated on Memorial Day 1893. *Courtesy of the Asbury Park Library.*

supposition to the post name, there is no evidence for this. Asbury Park veterans came from a number of areas in and out of New Jersey. Potts was, of course, originally a New Yorker, and the monument, as its inscription reveals, was generic in nature.

The statue itself was, according to Smithsonian Institution nineteenth-century statuary expert Carol Grissom, who reviewed modern photos, made of sheet copper and almost identical to one listed in the 1891 catalogue of the W.H. Mullins Company of Salem, Ohio. Mullins listed the statue at $300 for a six-foot-high version and $450 for a nine-foot-tall version.

The monument is guarded by two rare Dahlgren Heavy bronze twelve-pounder (so called because of the weight of the shot they fired) boat howitzers, named after their inventor, naval officer John A. Dahlgren. Dahlgren, an admiral during the Civil War, designed the guns, with their unique light iron frame carriages, in the wake of the Mexican War. He intended them to be mobile enough for use by naval landing parties and for easy movement on a ship's deck to repel enemy boarding parties. These artillery pieces were produced in various bore diameters, with bronze or iron barrels rifled and smooth-bored, and variously mounted on boat rail mountings and ship carriages, as well as the metal land carriages that hold the Asbury Park guns. Boat howitzers were often manned by sailors involved in amphibious landings to provide close-in artillery support for naval and marine landing parties. The Asbury Park examples were

The soldier statue atop the Civil War monument in 2012. *Courtesy of Joseph Bilby.*

manufactured for the navy in 1862 and are so marked. According to Civil War artillery expert Craig Swain, one of them was used on the steamer USS *Cricket* between 1862 and 1865.

Boat howitzers were also used by some army units, most notably the Seventy-first New York Infantry at Bull Run and the Ninth New York Infantry in the Maryland campaign of 1862. Some saw use as far inland as Arkansas by Indiana soldiers. They were used more frequently in coastal operations, however, especially by the First New York Marine Artillery.

In the late 1870s, the New Jersey National Guard dropped its two artillery batteries, replacing them with Gatling gun companies. In order to provide some artillery support to the infantry, National Guard infantry regiments were supplied with boat howitzers, manned by each regiment's separate "gun detachment." The detachments brought their howitzers to annual training at their Sea Girt campground somewhat south of Asbury Park and fired them at targets erected on rafts anchored four hundred yards from the beach.

There are decorative cannon barrels coupled with Civil War monuments all around New Jersey, but these are the only two boat howitzers. Why they were selected for the Asbury monument is unknown—perhaps because of its proximity to the ocean. In the mid-1880s, the National Guard Civil War–era muzzleloading howitzers were replaced by breech-loading guns, and it is possible that the Asbury Park artillery pieces were once National Guard weapons.

Over the years, several organizations, including the Sons of Union Veterans of the Civil War, heir to the Grand Army of the Republic, have petitioned the Asbury Park City Council to maintain the monument's artillery, which was beginning to sink into the

One of the boat howitzers located in the mini-park with the Asbury Park Civil War monument. *Courtesy of Joseph Bilby.*

ground and deteriorate. In 1999–2000, Clark McCullough and Robert V. McKnight of the George A. Custer Camp #17, Sons of Union Veterans, discussed this issue with representatives of the city and the New Jersey National Guard, with the result that the National Guard placed concrete slabs under the cannons' wheels, eliminating the possibility of sinking. There have been, over the years, some requests to remove the cannons from their positions at the monument and install them in a museum, where they would be protected from the elements (the iron carriages are quite rusty), although there has been no serious effort to implement this. The monument was rededicated in November 1999, with speakers, music and salutes from a Civil War artillery piece fired by Civil War reenactors as downtown Asbury Park, for the first time in its history, echoed with the fire of artillery.

Asbury Park is the only Monmouth County shore town to boast a Civil War monument, including, perhaps surprisingly, Long Branch, which was a major national resort at the time of the war, hosted Mary Lincoln in the summer of 1861, sent soldiers to fight in the war and was the summer home of such wartime luminaries as Ulysses S. Grant in the postwar era.

ABOUT THE AUTHORS

Joseph G. Bilby received his BA and MA degrees in history from Seton Hall University and served as a lieutenant in the 1st Infantry Division in Vietnam in 1966–67. He is retired from his position as supervising investigator for the New Jersey Department of Labor and is currently part-time assistant curator of the National Guard and Militia Museum of New Jersey in Sea Girt, New Jersey, and a freelance writer and historical consultant. He is the author, editor or coauthor of sixteen books and over four hundred articles on New Jersey history and folklore, military history and outdoor subjects, including *Asbury Park: A Brief History*, and is publications editor for the New Jersey Civil War Sesquicentennial Committee.

Harry Ziegler received his BA degree in English from Monmouth University and his ME from Georgian Court University. He worked for the *Asbury Park Press* for many years, rising to the position of managing editor. He is currently associate principal of Bishop George Ahr High School in Edison, New Jersey. Mr. Ziegler is coauthor of *Asbury Park: A Brief History* and *Hidden History of New Jersey*, both published by The History Press.

Visit us at
www.historypress.net